CHOREUTICS

THE UNIVERSITY OF
WINCHESTER

Martial Rose Library
Tel: 01962 827306

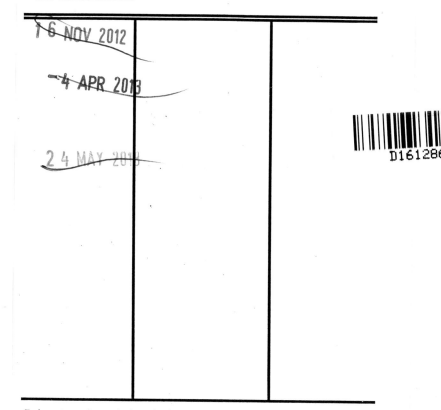

1 6 NOV 2012

- 4 APR 2013

2 4 MAY 2013

D1612869

To be returned on or before the day marked above, subject to recall.

CHOREUTICS

RUDOLF LABAN

Annotated and edited by

LISA ULLMANN

Dance Books • Alton

First published in 1966

This edition was published in 2011 by
Dance Books Ltd., Alton, Hampshire, UK

ISBN 978-185273148-9

To Dorothy and Leonard Elmhirst

Contents

Preface

"*Choreosophia*"—an ancient Greek word, from *choros*, meaning circle, and *sophia*, meaning knowledge or wisdom—is the nearest term I have discovered with which to express the essential ideas of this book. These ideas concern the wisdom to be found through the study of all the phenomena of circles existing in nature and in life. The term was used in Plato's time by the disciples and followers of Pythagoras. Although there is little real knowledge of the work of Pythagoras, we do know that about 540 B.C. he founded a philosophical and religious colony in Sicily, in which the cult of the Muses, the divine protectorates of the arts, seems to have played an important part. We do not know much about the fate of this Pythagorean community except that the surrounding population turned against the persistently grave demeanour of Pythagoras and his pupils. It is said that they were burnt alive together and that the colony's writings and works of art also perished in the flames, but the memory of Pythagoras is perpetuated by his discoveries in mathematics. One of these was the mathematics underlying musical scales, but best known is his theorem dealing with the harmonic relations of the different sides of a rectangular triangle.

Plato, in his *Timaeus*, and other contemporaries and disciples of the great philosopher give us a more exhaustive picture of the knowledge accumulated in the Pythagorean community, but this knowledge derives from even more remote times. The wisdom of circles is as old as the hills. It is founded on a conception of life and the becoming aware of it which has its roots in magic and which was shared by peoples in early stages of civilisation. Later religious, mystical and scientific epochs continued the tradition. The original conviction of the extraordinary role which the circle plays in harmony, life, and even in the whole of existence, survived the many changes in mentality, mood and feeling which abound in history.

Choreosophy seems to have been a complex discipline in the time of the highest Hellenic culture. Branches of the knowledge of circles came into being and were named "choreography," "choreology" and "choreutics." The first, choreography, means literally the designing or writing of circles. The word is still in use today: we call the planning and composition of a ballet or a dance "choreography." For centuries the word has been employed to designate the drawings of figures and symbols of movements which dance composers, or choreographers, jotted down as an aid to memory. There exist many systems, old and new, of dance notation and notation of movement in general, but most of them are restricted to a particular style of movement with which the writer and reader are familiar. Today we need a system of recording which can be universally used, and I have attempted to forge a way in this direction. My study of some hundred different forms of graphic presentation of characters of the different alphabets and other symbols, including those of music and dance, has helped me with the development of a new form of choreography which I called "kinetography." The system itself was inspired by that of Beauchamp and Fenillet (around 1700) and was mainly evolved alongside my investigations of the various branches of *choreosophia*.

The two other subjects of the knowledge of circles, choreology and choreutics, are not as well known as the first. Choreology is the logic or science of circles, which could be understood as a purely geometrical study, but in reality was much more than that. It was a kind of grammar and syntax of the language of movement, dealing not only with the outer form of movement but also with its mental and emotional content. This was based on the belief that motion and emotion, form and content, body and mind, are inseparably united. Finally, the third subject, choreutics, may be explained as the practical study of the various forms of (more or less) harmonised movement.

Movement is one of man's languages and as such it must be consciously mastered. We must try to find its real structure and the choreological order within it through which movement becomes penetrable, meaningful and understandable. In an attempt to do this, it has been found necessary to use various graphic signs, because words can never be entirely adequate in dealing with the changing nature of the subject before us. They are abstractions and, as it were, short cuts in the flow of life. Therefore, in order to gain a new aspect of movement and space, some elementary knowledge of choreography is needed, as through this the various choreutic elements can be identified.

In this book I have endeavoured to give a general survey of the central idea of choreutics, as well as a particular account of it. Because of an almost complete lack of knowledge about these things in the present day, it will be necessary for the reader to become quite clear about the first preliminaries, and this will demand a certain effort on his part. However, the choreographic, choreologic and choreutic matter through which I should like to lead the reader will, I hope, be more than a preparation, for when these aspects are both experienced and clearly understood, they are the real substance of the wisdom of circles.

*   *   *

The preceding paragraphs of this preface were written by Rudolf Laban as a preliminary to the present treatise. It was autumn 1939, the fateful month of the outbreak of the war. Laban worked with fervour on his book, which was intended to introduce himself and his ideas on movement and dance to an interested reading public in Britain. After a desolate year in Paris he had come to England in January, 1938 and found refuge at Dartington Hall. There Kurt and Aino Jooss, his friends and former pupils, helped him to regain his health, which had been very badly impaired by the devastating experiences he had suffered when his personal existence, as well as his life's work, was shattered by the Nazi régime in Germany. At nearly 60 years of age he had to start afresh. While still unable to work with people practically, he wished to contact them at least by writing about the basic trends of his thoughts on movement and the discoveries he had made in this field. But who would publish such a book? There was also the seemingly insurmountable problem of language. However, the latter difficulty found a temporary solution through the help of Louise Soelberg, the previous Director of the Dance Department at Dartington Hall and then member of the Ballets Jooss. I know Laban would wish me to record the gratitude he felt for the patience and devotion with which she struggled to make his English sound English.

By the time the manuscript had been brought to some degree of comprehensibility, the onset of war caused the closing down of the Arts Department at Dartington Hall (in June 1940) and with it the dispersal of its members, including Laban. Before leaving he dedicated his manuscript to Leonard and Dorothy Elmhirst and left it with them for safe keeping.

The ensuing years brought Laban better health as well as manifold opportunities for work with large numbers of people and thus for further discoveries and development of his ideas. No longer did he feel the need for a book containing solely his basic concepts, for other publications had come into being in which he had tried to show these applied to various fields of activity.

It was only several years after his death that Dorothy Elmhirst returned the manuscript to me with encouragement to have it published. This, together with my conviction that knowledge of the material is essential to the fuller understanding of Laban's work, has led me to prepare this book for the public. My only hesitation is a personal one, namely my limited ability as an editor. However, I hope the reader will bear with me for any clumsiness in presentation.

I have added a second part to Laban's original text, as I felt that a systematic survey of the grammatical elements of space-movement might help the student of movement and dance in his practical exercises. This part is entirely based on a compilation of the basic movement scales and configurations developed by Laban which was made by Gertrud Snell Friedburg, his former assistant, for his fiftieth birthday in 1929. The student may, however, be warned to resist the temptation of learning scales and configurations without thorough preparation. For a book can never replace the living teacher, and it is of no avail to acquire a mechanical skill in performance without the creative attitude which alone leads to deeper comprehension and thus to enrichment and growth. Laban's deliberations, together with his drawings in the first part of the book, cannot, I am sure, fail to inspire such an attitude, and I therefore consider it quite safe to publish the rudiments under their "umbrella."

I am greatly indebted to Betty Redfern, who read and re-read the draft of the first part and gave me invaluable help with the rendering of Laban's original text into the present form. I am grateful too for the generous assistance given me by several of my other colleagues who discussed and advised me on the illustrations and sections of the book.

LISA ULLMANN

Addlestone
January 1966

PART I

A New Aspect of Space and Movement

Introduction

OUR own movements and those we perceive around us are basic experiences. Forms of objects, as well as the shapes assumed by living organisms, wax and wane uninterruptedly. Yet forms of objects and living beings, when in quietude may suggest a "standstill" in the big unceasing stream of movement in which we exist and take part. This illusion of a standstill is based on the snapshot-like perception of the mind which is able to receive only a single phase of the uninterrupted flux. It is our memory which tends to perpetuate the illusion created by the "snapshots"; and the memory itself waxes, changes and vanishes.

Forms are closely connected with movement. Each movement has its form, and forms are simultaneously created with and through movement. The illusion of standstills creates an artificial separation of space and movement. Seen from such a point of view, space seems to be a void in which objects stand and—occasionally—move.

Empty space does not exist. On the contrary, space is a superabundance of simultaneous movements. The illusion of empty space stems from the snapshot-like perception received by the mind. What the mind perceives is, however, more than an isolated detail; it is a momentary standstill of the whole universe. Such a momentary view is always a concentration on an infinitesimal phase of the great and universal flux.

The sum of such snapshots is, however, not yet the flux itself. Cutting a film in pieces and heaping up the single pictures in a pile can never give the impression of a movement. Only when we let the pictures unroll does movement become visible. The unrolling snapshots can be shown in different ways. By mixing the snapshots in a higgledy-piggledy fashion, we shall obtain a fantastic picture as in a dream-world, full of unexpected jumps, breaks, gaps, overlaps and repetitions. The mind recognises the unreality of

3

such a film. A movement makes sense only if it progresses organically and this means that phases which follow each other in a natural succession must be chosen.

It is, therefore, essential to find out the natural characteristics of the single phases which we wish to join together in order to create a sensible sequence. We consider our snapshots separately only for the sake of analysing the characteristics of the whole flux. Looking at single snapshots, we must always feel and comprehend both the preceding and the following phase. Often it is necessary to be aware of connections leading even further back into the past or forward into the future of the flux of which the snapshot is a part.

The conception of space as a locality in which changes take place can be helpful here. However, we must not look at the locality simply as an empty room, separated from movement, nor at movement as an occasional happening only, for movement is a continuous flux within the locality itself, this being the fundamental aspect of space. Space is a hidden feature of movement and movement is a visible aspect of space.

In the past we have clung too stubbornly to a static conception of our environment, and consequently to a misconception of life in general, as well as of our own personal lives. Today we are perhaps still too accustomed to understanding objects as separate entities, standing in stabilised poses side by side in an empty space. Externally, it may appear so, but in reality continuous exchange and movement are taking place. Not for a moment do they come to a complete standstill, since matter itself is a compound of vibrations. We speak of movement only when we are aware of it as an uninterrupted stream. Extremely slow, weak or dispersed motions make us suppose that objects are in a state of rest, or immobile. This impression of rest is an illusion. What we cannot perceive with our senses, especially with our fundamental sense of touch (our tactile sense *see* Chapter III), remains unreal and its very existence is denied, until intuition or research discovers the unique and universal role of movement as a visible aspect of space.

It is possible to follow and to understand the continuous creation of spatial impressions through the experience of movement. The relationships between single spatial appearances cause movement to follow definite paths. The unity of movement and space can be demonstrated by comparing the single snapshots of the mind with each other, and showing that the natural order of their sequences and our natural orientation in space are based on similar laws.

When we wish to describe a single unit of space-movement we can adopt a method similar to that of an architect when drafting a building. He cannot show all the inner and outer views in one draft only. He is obliged to make a ground-plan, and at least two elevations, thus conveying to the mind a plastic image of the three-dimensional whole.

Movement is, so to speak, living architecture—living in the sense of changing emplacements as well as changing cohesion. This architecture is created by human movements and is made up of pathways tracing shapes in space, and these we may call "trace-forms." A building can hold together only if its parts have definite proportions which provide a certain balance in the midst of the continual vibrations and movements taking place in the material of which it is constructed. The structure of a building must endure shocks from alien sources, for instance, by the passing traffic, or by the jumping of lively inhabitants. The living architecture composed of the trace-forms of human movements has to endure other disequilibrating influences as they come from within the structure itself and not from without. The living building of trace-forms which a moving body creates is bound to certain spatial relationships. Such relationships exist between the single parts of the sequence. Without a natural order within the sequence, movement becomes unreal and dream-like.

Dream-architectures can neglect the laws of balance. So can dream-movements, yet a fundamental sense of balance will always remain with us even in the most fantastic aberrations from reality.

It is obvious that a dreamer and a man with a mind orientated towards mechanics will look upon movement differently. A different view will also be taken by those with a natural and unsophisticated mind—for instance, the child, or the so-called primitive man—who are not of an analytical mentality, but approach life in a simple and unified way.

The differing inner attitudes of individual personalities provide the different planes on which the snapshots can be projected. To begin with the most integrated attitude, we can state that children and the primitive man have both a natural gift for bodily movement and a natural love for it. In later periods of individual or racial life, man becomes cautious, suspicious, and sometimes even hostile to movement. He forgets that it is the basic experience of existence.

It is a curious fact that, not only for the searching mind of the scientist, but also for the child and the primitive man, the whole world is filled with unceasing movement. An unsophisticated mind has no difficulty in comprehending movement as life.

The personification of objects, and the belief that inorganic nature lives, have their source in the intuitive awareness of the universal and absolute presence of movement. This primitive view is an intuitive confirmation of the scientifically proved truth that what we call equilibrium is never complete stability or a standstill, but the result of two contrasting qualities of mobility.

Children and the man of primitive ages see the world through a bodily perspective, that is through physical experience. They see the amazing unity of all existence. Man of later times loses this view through his reflective delusions, and also because of his increasing tactile incapacity. He establishes stability in his mind as a contrasting partner to mobility. In this way he becomes unrelated to his surroundings which are, in the widest sense, the universe, and thus he loses his personality, which needs transgression from the I into the You so that he may be part of the harmonious order in the great and universal flux.

However, there have always been and still are people who are obliged to practise and observe movement more closely. In combat and work, people use their bodies extensively, while teachers of movement both experience and explain the rhythmical flow of changing trace-forms. In olden times the knowledge and practice of movement was kept alive by priests in the definite sequences and patterns of their religious rites, and later by dancing- and fencing-masters for social and educational purposes. Having, on the whole, a more simple and unsophisticated approach to motion, these people did not conceive that the measuring and analysing of movements and shapes would be such a complex undertaking. Time and again they attacked the problem courageously and even successfully in so far as their special practical needs were concerned.

One type of person will pay attention to movement only because of a pronounced distrust and aversion. Such people are more numerous than one would imagine. Anyone who seeks living reality in emotions and ideas alone is inclined to have a negative attitude towards bodily movement.

The opposite to the idea of the eternal stir of life is an abstract ideal of quietude, which to the convinced offers a world in which movement is reduced to an almost frozen form of harmony. People with this type of mind are an extreme contrast to the unsophisticated ones, who have a spontaneous feeling for movement.

Enthusiastic lovers of movement such as children and primitive peoples, as well as many lazy people, swim more or less contentedly in the same never-ceasing stream. The lazy ones, however, are less concerned with the pleasure and joy of movement, than with minimising the inconveniences and strain which any exertion causes them.

The above viewpoints represent degrees on a scale of temperaments of observers who unavoidably are in the same stream of existence but look at it from different angles. Such a scale obviously has more degrees than those described, but for our purpose, which is to find characteristic views offering a foundation for a multilateral description of movement, we may find it useful to select the following three aspects:

1. That of a mentality plunged into the intangible world of emotions and ideas.
2. That of the objective observer, from outside.
3. That of the person enjoying movement as bodily experience, and observing and explaining it from this angle.

These three aspects can be taken as the three views—the ground-plan and the two views of elevation—on which we project the image of the object of our investigations: the unit, movement and space.

A synthesis of these three aspects operates constantly in each one of us. We are all emotional dreamers, and scheming mechanics, and biological innocents, simultaneously: sometimes we waver between these three mentalities, and sometimes we compress them in a synthesised act of perception and function.

In endeavouring to make an analysis of movement, we must concern ourselves with the different layers of our inner life in which these three mentalities are rooted. Any description of movement must employ a concept, based on the different types of mentalities, and we can see that people who have studied movement have done this.

The following chapters contain, here and there, indications of the historical

2

attempt to invent a notation of movement. All these notations consisted of a compound of spatial relations and dynamic and rhythmic distinctions, as well as emotional characteristics of movement. The various qualities were united in a legible symbol signifying a single phase of its flow. As a generally known example music notation might be mentioned, in which symbols for the harmonic relations of sounds, rhythmic and dynamic sequences and expressive execution, form compounds through which the image of a musical movement is given. Choreographers (dance-writers) have followed a similar course when noting spatial and rhythmical movements of the body; they only added symbols for the limbs and other parts of the body.

A multilateral description of movement which views it from many angles is the only one which comes close to the complexity of the fluid reality of space. Thus in the following chapters, where movement cannot be described by words only, such choreographic symbols are used. In this way it is perhaps possible for space-movement to speak for itself.

The art, or the science, dealing with the analysis and synthesis of movement, we call "choreutics." Through its investigation and various exercises choreutics attempts to stop the progress of disintegrating into disunity. The bodily perspective, with all its significance for the human personality, can have a regenerating effect on our individual and social forms of life. Through constant and conscious usage this effect can be deepened, which helps us to explain the role that dance played in certain epochs of civilisation when a notable harmony was achieved.

To experience trace-forms from several viewpoints, integrating the bodily perspective, the dynamic feeling and the controlling faculties, necessitates a certain spiritual emphasis; this is unavoidable when penetrating into the real structure of human movement and motion in nature. The approach from different sides is, however, aimed at the discovery of a unity of movement. It is, without doubt, a fact that such a unity existed in ancient times in the paths of gestures which we have called trace-forms. Because it could not be explained, it assumed a magic significance and it is curious that even now it remains magical, in spite of being analysed.

Choreutics comprehends all kinds of bodily, emotional and mental movements and their notation. The choreutic synthesis embraces the various applications of movement to work, education and art, as well as to regenerative processes in the widest sense.

This aspect of space-movement can thus be called the "choreutic aspect." Rooted in practical experience as old as the hills, the choreutic aspect is, in spite of this, a new one. A definite awareness of it becomes especially important in our own time with its universal upheaval, and its love-hatred of motion in life, sciences and the arts.

CHAPTER I

Principles of Orientation in Space

MAN's movement arises from an inner volition which results in a transference of the body or one of its limbs from one spatial position to another. The outer shape of each movement can be defined by changes of position in space. Everyday terms of language suffice to describe, with precision, the position from which a movement starts, or the place to which it intends to go, and at which it finally arrives. The link between two positions is the "path" which the movement follows.

Wherever the body stays or moves, it occupies space and is surrounded by it. We must distinguish between space in general and the space within the reach of the body. In order to distinguish the latter from general space, we shall call it personal space or the "kinesphere." The kinesphere is the sphere around the body whose periphery can be reached by easily extended limbs without stepping away from that place which is the point of support when standing on one foot, which we shall call the "stance."* We are able to outline the boundary of this imaginary sphere with our feet as well as with our hands. In this way any part of the kinesphere can be reached. Outside the kinesphere lies the rest of space, which can be approached only by stepping away from the stance. When we move out of the limits of our original kinesphere we create a new stance, and transport the kinesphere to a new place. We never, of course, leave our movement sphere but carry it always with us, like an aura.

When we take a step forward, we carry our kinesphere the length of a step forward through space. The stance is always beneath the point of equilibrium of the body, never at the side or in front, or behind it. We feel each stance as a part of ourself, and each new movement grows from it.

* Sometimes called "place."

The basic elements of orientation in space are the three dimensions: length, breadth and depth. Each "dimension" has two directions. With reference to the human body, length, or height, has the two directions up and down; breadth has the two directions left and right; depth has the two directions forward and backward. The centre of gravity of the upright body is approximately the dividing point between the two directions of each dimension. Thus this point becomes, as well, the centre of our kinesphere.

The three-dimensional form composed of height, breadth and depth, which is the easiest to visualise, is the cube. Oblique lines, which may be called "diagonals" of space, lead from each corner of the cube to the opposite corner, and each is a kind of axis, which is surrounded by three dimensions. There are four such space diagonals in the cube, and they intersect at a point in the body which coincides approximately with its centre of gravity, which is also the centre of our kinesphere as has been mentioned above.

These four diagonals do not have such clearly defined names as the dimensions. In general they are named by the three surrounding dimensions; for instance, a diagonal may lead towards high, right, forward, and in the opposite direction, deep, left, backward.

We also distinguish axes which lie between two diagonals and two dimensions. We may call them "diameters" and consider them to be "deflected" from the dimensions or from the diagonals. There are six such diameters in the cube and they also intersect roughly at the centre of gravity.

The six diameters, again, have no clearly defined names in everyday language. They can be described, however, by the two dimensions between which they lie. For instance, a diameter lying between high and right side leads towards high-right, and in the opposite direction, deep-left. It is only in the art of movement, and particularly in dance, that these spatial relations need to be precisely defined, and as a first step towards the understanding of the new aspect of movement we employ the terminology of the dancer to describe relations of positions in space.

In the well-known five positions in dance, the dancer places his feet and his body either in the directions of the three dimensions, or in the diagonal directions between them. In the first position the feet are placed with the heels together and toes apart. It is this position which creates the stance.

Movements directed towards the stance lead downward. In the second position the feet are placed apart sideways, on a line extending between the left and right dimensional directions. In the third position the feet are placed at an angle, with the heel of one foot by the instep of the other. The feet indicate an oblique line lying between the two spatial extensions of depth and breadth; for instance, between forward and right, and backward and left. In the fourth position the feet are placed apart one behind the other, on a line extending between the forward and backward directions. In the fifth position the feet are placed closely one behind the other. In this position no special direction is accentuated except perhaps that of upward because of a tendency to stretch the whole body in this situation. We employ the fifth position, therefore, as the position which is symbolic of height.

With regard to the positions of the legs and arms, when in the air, there is no uniform tradition. In the movement notation which the author has developed, and which has been used for some time in the fields of dance, work and education, the directions of the positions of the legs and arms, when in the air, correspond to the general directions of the aforesaid five classical positions of the feet.

Three different spatial levels may be distinguished: one on the floor, another at the mid-height of the body, and the third at the height of the hands, when raised above the head. The following names and symbols can be used, in order to make the directions clear:

The notation symbol for the direction downward towards the stance is:

deep: ▊

The direction symbol upward towards above the head is:

high: ▯

The direction symbols towards the sides of the body are as follows:

at medium level:	*at high level:*	*at low level:*
right: ▷	high right: ▷	deep right: ▶
left: ◁	high left: ◁	deep left: ◀

The symbols for directions directly in front of or behind the body are as follows:

at medium level:	at high level:	at low level:
forward: 🯄	high forward: 🯄	deep forward: 🯄
backward: 🯄	high backward: 🯄	deep backward: 🯄

The symbols for the four oblique directions are:

at medium level:	at high level:	at low level:
right forward: 🯄	high right forward: 🯄	deep right forward: 🯄
right backward: 🯄	high right backward: 🯄	deep right backward: 🯄
left forward: 🯄	high left forward: 🯄	deep left forward: 🯄
left backward: 🯄	high left backward: 🯄	deep left backward: 🯄

The above 26 directions radiate from the centre of the kinesphere, the 27th point of direction (🯄), and establish three planes each at different levels: high, medium, low.

Figs. 1, 2, 3 and 4 show the different spatial crosses in relation to these planes.

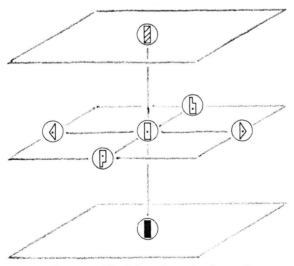

FIG. 1.—*The "three-dimensional cross."*

Fig. 1 shows the "three-dimensional cross." It is formed by the six principal directions:

$$▨ \quad ▮ \quad ◁ \quad ▷ \quad ▯ \quad ◖$$

radiating from the common centre of the body and its kinesphere, ▯. We call these "dimensional directions."

Each dimensional direction or "ray"* lies between four directions or rays of the diagonal cross; for instance:

$$▨$$

lies as a kind of axial point between:

$$◗ \quad ▨ \quad ◆ \quad ▨$$

Fig. 2 shows the "four-diagonal cross." It is formed by the eight diagonal

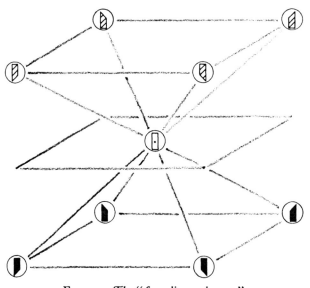

FIG. 2.—*The "four-diagonal cross."*

---

* Movements radiating from and to the common centre of the body and its kinesphere may be called "rays."

directions,

radiating from the common centre of the body and its kinesphere, ⊡ . We call these diagonals "diagonal inclinations"* and their directions: "diagonal directions."

Each diagonal direction or ray lies between three directions or rays of the dimensional cross; for instance: ⬘ lies as a kind of axis between: ⬘ ⬘ ◁ .

Fig. 3 shows the "six-diametral cross." It is formed by the twelve deflected directions:

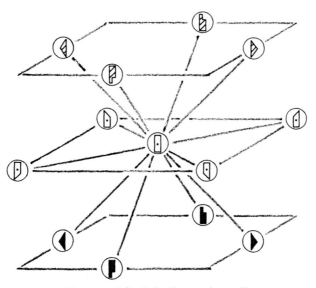

FIG. 3.—*The "six-diametral cross."*

* The term "inclination" is introduced to denote a digression from the given norm, the three-dimensional cross, caused by another spatial influence.

radiating from the common centre of the body and its kinesphere, ⏹ . We call these diameters "diametral inclinations" or primary deflected inclinations* and their directions "diametral directions."

Each diametral direction lies between two rays of the dimensional cross, and two rays of the diagonal cross; for instance:

ⴱ

lies in the centre of the four rays:

ⴱ ⴱ ⴱ ⴱ

Fig. 4 shows three levels of a cube in relation to:
    (*a*) the dimensional cross,
    (*b*) the diagonal cross,
    (*c*) the diametral cross.

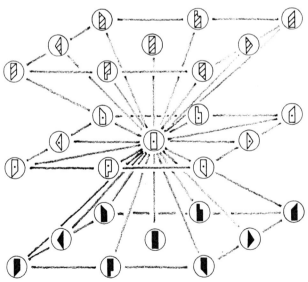

FIG. 4.—*The main directional rays establishing three levels in cubic space.*

* See secondary deflected inclinations on p. 68.

Actually, the six diameters or primary deflected inclinations are those which we most easily distinguish when seeing and experiencing movement. We can continue the deflecting of the original six dimensional and eight diagonal directions, and there is no end to this process, for the number of possible inclinations is infinite.

First fact of space-movement

Innumerable directions radiate from the centre of our body and its kinesphere into infinite space.

CHAPTER II

The Body and the Kinesphere

EXTENSION in space is a fundamental function of matter. Living matter is organised in bodily units, and has, apart from the natural extension in growth, the gift of extending and contracting these bodily units. Such a bodily unit is the body of a moving person; it follows the inner impulse of a mysterious autonomic will. The directions of contraction and extension can vary, and they are chosen and altered by volition. The human body is constructed so as to favour the extension and contraction of the limbs in certain directions, but all points of the kinesphere can be reached by simple movements, such as bending, stretching and twisting, or by a combination of these. The spheric form of the kinesphere is simplified by our cubic conception of space. We recognise the cube inside the kinesphere as being representative of the most important space directions. The intrinsic construction of the human body, however, shows a much simpler form than a cube.

The simple one-dimensional vertical (or when the body lies on the floor, the horizontal) is the fundamental structural extension of the body. It is interesting that, when moving, we think of the direction of our head as height, and of the direction of our feet as depth. It is the beginning of an intellectual complication when we transpose this primary feeling to the dimensions relative to the earth's centre of gravity, and to our surroundings, instead of to our own construction.

The second extension which we feel originates from the bilateral organisation of our body, caused by the mirror-like structure of the left and right sides. The vertical extension together with the bilateral extension give a two-dimensional feeling. (This is expressed in the dancer's idea of the "second position.") Seen from this point of view, we are flat beings, resembling the plane-like formation of the leaves of plants (*see* Fig. 5). The plasticity of the body is only slightly accentuated by its anatomical construction and the third dimension becomes apparent only when moving; usually in everyday life when stepping or reaching and grasping, and manipulating objects (*cf.* the dancer's "fourth position").

Between the bilateral bodily extension and movement into the third dimension, there is a transitional stage which leads to the diagonal directions (*cf.* the dancer's "third position"). This stage comes about because we turn one side of our body slightly towards our goal when stepping or reaching forward in grasping, thus giving up the two-dimensional character of our bilateral structure. In this way one side becomes active and the other remains more or less restful, or passive.

Our flat bodily structure encourages a division into five principal zones: the zone of the head, the two zones of the arms, and the two zones of the legs.

Fig. 5 shows an elementary posture. Both *feet* support the weight of the body in the corresponding directions of:

◀ and ▶ ;

both *arms* are spread in the corresponding directions of:

◁ and ▷ ;

and the *head* is carried straight upward in the direction:

▯

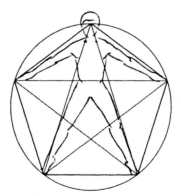

Fig. 5.—*A flat pentagonal pose of the body.*

Our body, in this pentagonal pose, is like a star with five equal pulls towards five points of the kinesphere. Sometimes an awareness of the extended arms and legs prevails, when the arms are somewhat raised and tension is particularly stressed in the extremities. We then become less conscious of the vertical direction, but have rather the feeling of a quadrangular construction. This tension tends to evoke a more ecstatic feeling than that accompanying the pentagonal attitude, which seems to arouse a state of intellectual awareness.

An interesting spatial tension occurs in flying through the air when the movement is characterised by a four-directional pull. For instance, one leg might go downwards towards the stance ▮, the other leg extending into an oblique direction ▯, and the arms stretching into directions ▯ and ▯ in the upper plane. This tension has the form of a tetrahedron, which is the simplest plastic form having four corners. The feeling of plasticity is sometimes enhanced by a movement of the head and trunk arching backwards.

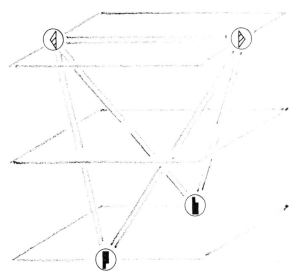

FIG. 6.—*A tetrahedral form representing plasticity of a bodily pose.*

Fig. 6 shows a regular tetrahedron arising from the forward-backward position of the feet and the sideways-upward directions of the arms. Almost all positions of the body can be reduced or related to a tetrahedral form for they are plastic variations of the flat quadrangle. The fundamental poses in the sacred dances of Oriental peoples frequently show regular five-cornered, quadrangular or tetrahedral forms.

The spatial tension of a plastic pose or movement of the whole body can be recognised in the following ways:

1. *Four directions.* When supported by one leg one of these directions is always self-evident, because it leads towards the stance and can, therefore, be left out of account. Thus we have to deal only with a three-directional movement or pose.

2. *Five directions.* Discounting again the one towards the stance, only a four-directional movement or pose can be distinguished.

3. *Six and more directions.* A movement in flight is likely to be many-directional, but here as in other complicated movements we often need a series of secondary tensions executed by smaller parts of the body, its limbs, or its trunk. In these many-directional movements a tetrahedral kernel can, nevertheless, be recognised as the simplest expression of the whole tension.

The change from one pose to another can be done in two different ways. Either one limb or one part of the body at a time moves into a new space direction, or two or more limbs or parts of the body perform the change in space simultaneously. The first kind of movement is "monolinear," the second "polylinear." A sequence of either creates pathways in space. These paths can be closed lines, which may be called "circuits," or "rings," since they return to their starting point, or open lines or curves which lead from one point of the kinesphere to another.

The path of a movement can originate from any part or zone of the kinesphere, and lead to any other part of it. We speak about zones, and not about directional points only, because the movements of the body and its limbs do not generally make straight lines, but form curves, passing through zones which are an accumulation of points situated on the circumference of the kinesphere.

Each limb has its own zone, which is that part of the kinesphere which can be reached by moving only the limb in question, without much additional movement. A trained dancer can lift his leg very high, sometimes to the dimensional ray ▯, but the normal zone of the leg does not include such extraordinary extensions, which can be reached only by special training, or individual aptitude.

The normal zone of the right leg can be seen in a circuit following the directions: d, df, f, rf, r, rb, b, db and returning finally to d (*see* Fig. 7). This line may be expressed as follows:

$$ \blacksquare \cdots \blacksquare \cdots \boxed{\natural} \cdots \boxed{d} \cdots \triangleright \cdots \boxed{\natural} \cdots \boxed{p} \cdots \blacksquare \cdots \mid \blacksquare $$

NOTE: the stroke | is employed as a kind of bar-line, marking the beginning or the ending of a movement. The dots after the directional symbols mean the continuity of the movement. They can also be employed to mark the duration in time. The number of dots between the directional signs would then indicate the number of time units.

The circuit shown in Fig. 7 is called the "normal zone of the right leg." In the terminology of classical ballet it is known as a "rond de jambe."

The normal zone of the left leg has a corresponding circuit on the other side of the body:

$$ \blacksquare \cdots \blacksquare \cdots \boxed{\natural} \cdots \boxed{\natural} \cdots \triangleleft \cdots \boxed{p} \cdots \boxed{p} \cdots \blacksquare \cdots \mid \blacksquare $$

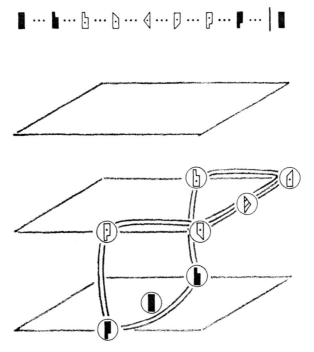

FIG. 7.—*Normal zone of the right leg.*

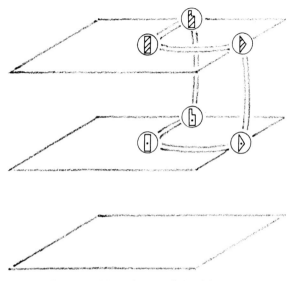

FIG. 8.—*Normal zone of the right arm.*

Fig. 8 shows a circuit outlining the normal zone of the right arm:

This appears in a gesture, known in ballet terminology as a "port de bras." The left arm has a corresponding circuit, outlining its zone, on the other side of the body.

Fig. 9 illustrates a zone easily followed by the trunk:

This ring is the prototype of a tetragonal or quadrangular circuit which changes direction four times.

With each limb we can follow the outline of three, four, five, six, seven, eight and more cornered zones. Combining the movements of trunk and limbs, we reach points which cover an area much wider than the normal zone, and thus we form the "super-zone."

Bending, and at the same time turning the trunk downward to the right side, we can reach with our right hand ▶ and then, moving the body together

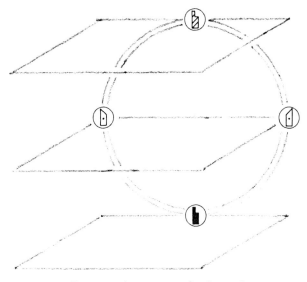

FIG. 9.—*An easy zone for the trunk.*

with the right arm by lifting and twisting the trunk, we reach without difficulty the six-cornered (hexagonal) super-zone. This is illustrated in Fig. 10,
which shows the circuit:

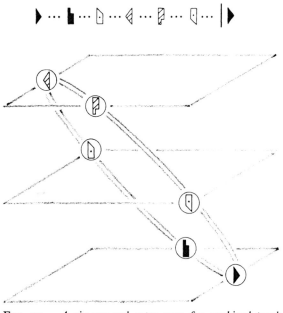

FIG. 10.—*A six-cornered super-zone for combined trunk
and arm movement.*

A closed line, or ring, which bounds a seven-cornered super-zone of the right arm is shown in Fig. 11, which illustrates the circuit:

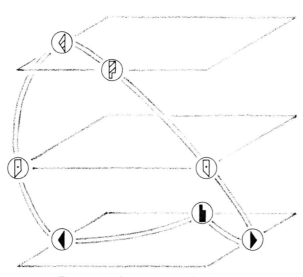

FIG. 11.—*A seven-cornered super-zone.*

This super-zone, formed by seven separate directions, gives the basis for a harmonic order of the inclinations. We call such rings "heptagonal" chains or circuits.

It is obvious that the legs also have super-zones. For instance, the circuit shown in Fig. 12 is an octagonal super-zone of the right leg; this may be given by:

Our body is constructed in a manner which enables us to reach certain points of the kinesphere with greater ease than others. An intensive study of the relationship between the architecture of the human body and its pathways in space facilitates the finding of harmonious patterns. Knowing the rules of the harmonic relations in space we can then control and form the flux of our motivity.

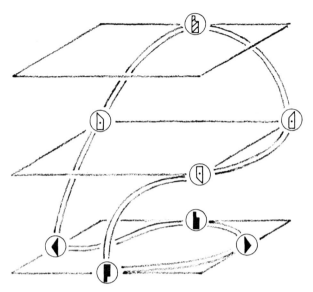

FIG. 12.—*An eight-cornered super-zone for the right leg.*

This science of harmonic circles has its origin in the discovery of the laws which rule the architecture of the body. It is obvious that harmonious movement follows the circles which are most appropriate to our bodily construction.

Our mind seems to conceive and understand space in the light of these structural laws. We also discover that the same laws rule not only the construction of living beings but also the structure of all inorganic matter and its crystallisation. With this discovery the whole of nature may be recognised as being governed by the same choreutic laws, the laws of interdependent circles.

Second fact of space-movement

Our body is the mirror through which we become aware of ever-circling motions in the universe with their polygonal rhythms. Polygons are circles in which there is spatial rhythm, as distinct from time rhythm. A triangle accentuates three points in the circumference of a circle, a quadrangle four points, a pentagon five points, and so forth. Each accent means a break of the circuit line, and the emergence of a new direction. These directions follow one another with infinite variations, deflections and deviations.

CHAPTER III

Exploration of the Dynamosphere

THE study of movement deals with the spatial order of the paths which the limbs make in the kinesphere, and also with the connection between outer movement and the mover's inner attitude. This attitude is not only shown in the choice of a certain path or the employment of a certain limb, but is also characterised by the choice of dynamic stresses.

Movements can be executed with differing degrees of inner participation and with greater or lesser intensity. They may be accelerated by an exaggerated desire to reach a goal or retarded by a cautious doubting attitude. The mover may be entirely concentrated on a movement and use the whole body in an act of powerful resistance, or casually employ only part of the body with delicate touch. Thus we get different dynamic qualities. One of the basic experiences of the dynamics of movement is that its different spatial nuances always show clearly distinguishable mental and emotional attitudes. It is possible to relate the moving person's feeling for dynamics to the spatial harmonics within trace-forms and to the zones through which the paths of the trace-forms lead.

Some of the simplest correlations of space and expression can be described and comprehended without any knowledge of fundamental spatial laws. For instance, when a movement is accompanied by a secondary one in another part of the body in an opposite spatial direction, it can easily be understood that the secondary movement might inhibit or disturb the main movement; it might diminish its speed, decrease its dynamic power and deviate its direction. Sometimes in this way dynamic nuances can be explained by the spatial influence of secondary movements and tensions

Each movement takes a certain time for its completion and we distinguish, in each movement, different phases of its pathway. One part of it vanishes into the past, a second part is momentarily present, and a third part will presumably follow, and complete the movement. After this third phase, the movement disappears. Its trace remains only in the memory or, externally, in a change of the place of an object in space, or in a new position of the limbs of the body. Innumerable positions are constantly produced and changed; when a new position appears the former one has disappeared. This flux of time can, therefore, be understood as an infinite number of changing situations. Since it is absolutely impossible to take account of each infinitesimal part of movement we are obliged to express the multitude of situations by some selected "peaks" within the trace-form which have a special quality. The most characteristic, of course, are those which strike us by their spatial appearance, but we must remain aware of the fact that those selected for description are connected with one another by numberless transitory positions.

Besides the innumerable changing situations in a movement there are also endless possibilities of its inclination as well as variation of its trace-forms (*see end of* Chapters I and II). In fact, we are able to make an infinite number of trace-forms and each of these trace-forms consists of an infinite number of single parts or situations. These two infinities must be taken into consideration when we wish to understand and describe movement.

The first of these infinities (the infinite number of trace-forms) can be understood as a kind of reservoir, from which the second infinity (the infinite number of single parts) is created by the selection of situations appropriate to the intended movement. Thus the path of movement contains countless positions in space with several outstanding characteristic peaks between its appearance and final disappearance. We might also say that the path consists of an infinite number of appearances and disappearances, which we called the flux of time. Although we can experience the wholeness of a trace-form when we move, we cannot grasp all its details unless we examine each part bit by bit.

All that we perceive through our eyes consists of objects or movements arranged in space. So it is with our aural perception, or hearing. Sounds are spatial arrangements, vibrations or oscillations, and they fade from our ears in the same way that visible movements vanish before our eyes. We can see different movements or hear different sounds at the same time. For instance, in a rainbow different colours are seen placed side by side, each representing a certain number of oscillations of light rays. We perceive the different kinds of sense excitement through vibrations which are communicated to our eyes by the curious condition of space in which sight is possible and which we call light.

In all these phenomena we can see that the number of vibrations in a certain unit of time varies in regular proportion, which means that one colour or one sound has a certain number of vibrations, another can have a double, triple, quadruple, etc., number. Relations of vibrations expressed in primary numbers give our senses an impression of balance which we call harmony. For instance, the octave in music has the relation 1:2 which means that the vibrations of the high octave are twice as many as the lower one. There is also a numerical relationship between the primary colours of red, blue and yellow and it is the purpose of this investigation to point out the possibility of discovering similar relations in the trace-forms of movement.

In comparing durations of movements we use a conventional unit of time, the second, which corresponds approximately to one heart-beat. This is a contraction of a part of the body and is, therefore, an act of a body part causing change in space. All changes in space which we see, hear, smell or taste are literally tactile impressions. All our senses are variations of our unique sense of touch. Two approaching objects touch one another when they finally meet without a noticeable space between them. They collide in this way. This is what happens in any condensing matter in which the outer parts move towards a centre, as for instance in crystallisation. Each single part of matter approaches its neighbouring part until the two collide, causing an impact or a pressure. It is space which appears and disappears between and around objects and in the movements of the particles of the object.

As already stated, the kinesphere is that part of space which can be reached with the extremities. The divisions of the kinesphere which one conceives and feels as the places above or below the centre of the body, or to its left or right, are all possible targets of movement. The zones of the kinesphere become apparent and are felt at the moment when they are touched by the moving body.

Intensity, tension, weight and energy which the different contractions of the body communicate to our perceptive faculties are different terms for another fundamental function of space, that of condensation. Condensation in space gives us the impression of a single peak, or selected part, within the infinite flux of time, which is in fact disappearing space. It gives us the capacity to produce new positions, encounters and percussions, new contacts and possibilities of tactile experiences both within the body itself and in relation to its surroundings. This capacity is muscular energy or force.

As different manifestations in space, force and time have complicated connections. Traditional ways of the observation and teaching of movement have, however, led to relatively simple descriptions of these. In dancing, a terminology has been evolved for the most obvious manifestations in space. Elementary contrasts between basic forms of dynamic movements have been found, such as beating, slashing and gliding which are called in the French ballet terminology *battu, fouetté*, and *glissé*.

There are a large number of variations of natural dynamic activities. They can be arranged in groups just as can directions, dimensions and inclinations, and we may notice connections between certain directions in space, especially those of the diagonals, and fundamental dynamic actions. Besides slashing and gliding, others such as pressing, wringing, floating, punching, flicking, dabbing, are everyday actions with a clear dynamic meaning. In that part of the study of choreutics which we called eukinetics* the dynamic structure of these movements can be exactly determined. The result is a scheme which is comparable to that of orientation in space. The space in which our dynamic actions take place may be called the "dynamosphere."

The body and its limbs are able to execute certain dynamic nuances in movement towards certain areas in space better than towards others. The locations most advantageous for the principal dynamic exertions can be represented in a cube. The following is an attempt to show that this cube of the dynamosphere can be correlated with the cube of the kinesphere.

It is not possible to provide a completely comprehensive explanation of the dynamic actions in terms of time and force only. A third conception must be used which derives from spatial influences.

Six elementary distinctions thus emerge and experience shows that they have a definite correlation with the six fundamental directions in space: up and down, left and right, backward and forward. When we move into these

* Laban introduced this term many years ago when he explored the laws of harmony within kinetic energy. Later he expanded this field of study and called it "effort" and the above-mentioned eight activities became known as the eight basic effort actions.

directions a kind of secondary tendency appears in the body, namely a dynamic quality which is not always clearly definable by the spectator but is very real to the mover.

One can set down the following scheme:

1. A feeling of lightness, of losing strength, corresponds with the reaching upward to the point where the arm or the body prepares to relax and to fall back towards the ground. Therefore, lightness is correlative with a tendency upward.

2. A strong, firm movement always has at its source a vital connection with the stance. We can easily feel that every strong movement is correlated to a foothold downwards. Therefore, strength is correlative with a tendency downward.

3. Movement across the body brings about a spatial restriction for the moving limb which makes for confined use of space. Therefore a straight, direct movement is correlative with one leading to the lateral direction opposite to the moving part of the body.

4. Movement of the limb on its own side brings about a spatial freedom which makes for a roundabout and flexible use of space. Therefore, flexibility is correlative with an opening outwards.

5. A quick, sudden movement is connected with a certain contraction. The natural direction of contraction in the whole body tends to be backward as seen, for instance, in shock when jerks of fright cause the central area of the body to retract. Therefore quick, sudden tensions are correlative with movements into a backward direction.

6. A slow movement seems to release into the opposite direction, namely into the area in front and, therefore, slowness and sustainment are correlative with reaching into a forward direction.

This simplified scheme forms the basis for certain correlations of dynamic nuances with spatial directions and this reciprocal relationship rules harmonious movement in the kinesphere. What should be understood, however, is that the correlation of dimensional movements with dynamic stresses is most strongly felt in freely-flowing movement, whereas if the flow is restrained different correlations arise.

Movements of any dynamic shade can, of course, be made into any desired direction, but as a basic training it is valuable to perform:

1. Light movements (in which the body or
   parts of it are carried with the slightest
   possible tension)   . . . into upward directions.

2. Strong movements (which firmly stress
   resistance to gravity)   . . . into downward direc-
                                                                         tions.

3. Straight movements (which reach their
   goal in an undeviating direct manner)   . . . into sideways (crossed)
                                                                 directions.

4. Roundabout movements (in which spatial
   freedom is achieved through flexibility
   of the body)   . . . into sideways (open)
                                                                      directions.

5. Quick movements (which suddenly effect
   a change of position)   . . . into backward direc-
                                                                         tions.

6. Slow movements (in which continuity is
   sustained for a relatively long period)   . . . into forward directions.

Compounds of these which form the eight fundamental dynamic actions
evolve in areas of the dynamosphere which correspond approximately to the

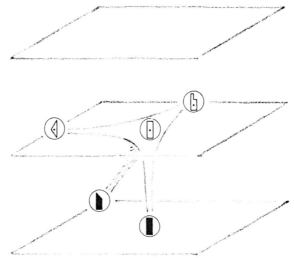

FIG. 13.—*Kinespheric direction of "pressing" with a right limb.*

eight diagonal directions of the kinesphere. They create "secondary" trace-forms which can be indicated by using the directional signs of the kinesphere and adding the letter "S."

Fig. 13 shows the kinespheric direction of the dynamic action of pressing performed by a right limb.

In *pressing* (or pushing) a concentrated force is maintained in which the movement is relatively

$$\left.\begin{array}{l} \text{slow} \\ \text{strong} \\ \text{straight} \end{array}\right\} \text{S}$$

The area into which the pressure is exerted by the right side of the body is around the diagonal ▌ which is the axis of the three rays:

Pressing as a secondary trace-form may, therefore, be expressed by the symbol of the corresponding diagonal ▌ₛ

In a *wringing* (or pulling) action for the right side of the body the movement is relatively

$$\left.\begin{array}{l} \text{slow} \\ \text{strong} \\ \text{roundabout} \end{array}\right\} \text{S} \qquad \text{Expressed by the symbol of the corresponding diagonal: ▌ₛ}$$

Gliding is a smooth caressing kind of movement, which is relatively

$$\left.\begin{array}{l} \text{slow} \\ \text{light} \\ \text{straight} \end{array}\right\} \text{S} \qquad \text{Expressed by the symbol of the corresponding diagonal: ▨ₛ}$$

Floating is a gently stirring kind of movement which is relatively

$$\left.\begin{array}{l} \text{slow} \\ \text{light} \\ \text{roundabout} \end{array}\right\} \text{S} \qquad \text{Expressed by the symbol of the corresponding diagonal: ▨ₛ}$$

These represent four slow, sustained actions. Terms for them are not easily found because our language is not rich in clearly defined words for movements and actions, especially for those which express the experience of a moving person. Quick actions are even more difficult to describe in words. This is one of the principal reasons why a notation of movement through symbols is necessary. There are two, however, which are comparatively easily understood. These are "slashing" and "punching."

Slashing is a rapid action made at random which is relatively

> quick
> strong   S   The symbol of the corresponding
> roundabout   diagonal is:

Punching is an effectively aimed quick action which is relatively

> quick
> strong   S   The symbol of the corresponding
> straight   diagonal is:

The two quick and light movements which might be called "dabbing" and "flicking" are as follows:

Dabbing is a vibratory patting kind of action which is relatively

> quick
> light   S   The symbol for the corresponding
> straight   diagonal is:

Flicking is a jerky flapping kind of action which is relatively

> quick
> light   S   The symbol for the corresponding
> roundabout   diagonal is:

Further combinations such as those contained in the deflected directions can be developed in the dynamosphere in exactly the same way. The possibilities of combination go on endlessly. For simple practical purposes the relationships enumerated in this chapter suffice. They are the nuances which can be most easily distinguished. Every trace-form has hidden dynamic connections which are followed intuitively by the moving person. To unveil these hidden relations is one of the aims of the study of choreutics and the art of movement.

The general rhythmic and dynamic qualities of a movement can be recorded in musical signs. Signs such as ♪♩ 𝅗𝅥 show the relative duration of the parts of an action and the bar-lines indicate the placement of stress and non-stress within its sequence. There is, however, a lack in music notation of any hint of the spatial quality of movement in the sense of direct or flexible progression. The need for this is met by movement notation which includes indications of the rhythmic and dynamic qualities and provides a mode of recording movement sequences of a complex nature.

When examining the rhythm of a movement we have also to consider the tempo; that is, the variations between rapidity and slowness. In playing a musical instrument we clearly feel rapidity in such sound-producing movements as whipping, thrusting, tapping and plucking, and slowness in pulling, gliding, floating and pressing actions.

Certain musical signs and terms such as *sostenuto, presto, forte, piano, glissando, staccato*, etc., indicate the mood of these actions in the dynamospheric sense, which means the kind of bodily tension with which the instrument is to be played.

When we work, play, dance, fight and so forth we use the body as the instrument. The handling of this instrument can be directed either by our feeling and taste or by some suggestion or definite indication of the main characteristics of each movement which can be given through movement notation.

The notation of dynamospheric and kinespheric trace-forms denotes the expressive nature of actions as well as their outward attributes. However, the inner meaning of movement can perhaps be described by special dynamospheric symbols still more explicitly than by spatial ones or even by words since we cannot say that movement forms with dynamospheric tendencies are always derivatives of those in kinetic space. The contrary could also be the case.

Third fact of space-movement

Although dynamospheric currents are secondary in respect of their spatial visibility, they may be regarded as the primary factor in the actual generating of our movements; that is, the generating of visible spatial unfoldings and definite directional sequences with which they form a unity. In reality they are entirely inseparable from each other. It is only the amazing number of possible combinations which, in order to comprehend them, makes it necessary for us to look at them from two distinct angles, namely that of form and that of dynamic stress.

CHAPTER IV

Natural Sequences and Scales in Space

A SERIES of natural sequences of movements exists which we follow in our various everyday activities. Such sequences, which seem to have been consciously used since the earliest days of civilisation, are determined by the anatomical structure of our body. These sequences, or scales, always link the different zones of the body and its limbs in a logical way. In everyday activity movement has a practical purpose, for instance, in pushing the water away in swimming, or in attacking an opponent and defending ourselves when fighting. In sword fencing especially, we notice a very clear sequence of six movements which correspond closely to our fundamental orientation in space.

In every kind of fighting observed in nature certain features of defence may be noticed, since all highly organised beings have several particularly vulnerable regions of the body. These regions are:

1. The organs of the senses concentrated in the head.
2. The right flank between the hip-bone and the ribs.
3. The jugular vein on the left side of the neck.
4. The right jugular vein.
5. The left flank.
6. The abdomen.

Man protects these six vulnerable regions by six special movements.

1. The defence of the head necessitates raising the right arm upwards vertically: ▯ .
2. The defence of the right flank demands a lateral movement downwards: ▮ .
3. The left jugular vein is protected by a movement of the right arm across to the left: ◁ .

4. The right jugular vein is protected by forcing the aggressor's weapon sideways to the right: ▷ .

5. The left flank is guarded by a backward movement across the body fending off the aggressor's weapon: ⊡ .

6. The abdomen is shielded by an advancing movement, repulsing the aggressor: ♮ .

It is assumed in this description that the defender holds the right side of his body forward. Usually a man exposes to an adversary the smallest surfaces of his trunk, and these are his sides, the human body being built in a flat plane resembling the leaves of a plant, as already mentioned in Chapter II. Right-handed people will fight with the right arm, thus advancing the right side.

The movements of defence (called in fencing, parrying) are arranged in a definite sequence which is identical with the above description. The parry number one is called in fencing, "prime." This is the raising of the right arm. The parry number two is called "second," which is the lowering of the right arm. The "third" parry is the bringing of the right arm inwards to the left; the "fourth," the lifting of the right arm outwards to the right; the "fifth," the moving of the right arm backward across the left side of the body; and the "sixth" striking forward with the right arm.

The right arm swings through this sequence in the following order:

▨ ···	▮ ···	◁ ···	▷ ···	⊡ ···	♮ ··· │ ▨
upward	downward	inward (left)	outward (right)	backward	forward upward

(Instead of left and right, the expression inwards and outwards is used to correspond to the bodily feeling during the movement.)

A left-handed man would use his left arm in defence and attack, and would advance his left side. He would execute the same sequence in a mirror-like way with the left arm.

The attack is the counterpart of the defence. The blows proceed towards the central area of the adversary's body from the circumference of his kinesphere; for instance, the attack on the head comes from above.

It is interesting to look upon the thrusts and parries of two opponents as an interplay between their respective kinespheres. The general spatial orientation of the attacker shows a confluence of his movements approximately in front of himself no matter from which area they come. The spatial orientation of the defender is dispersed into a number of directions of his kinesphere. The kinesphere of the one will at times overlap with that of the other since the attacker will always attempt to reach his opponent's body with his strokes, often involving one or more steps towards it.

The fundamental orientation in space of the defender's parrying actions is given by directions radiating from his centre towards:

⬚ ▮ ◁ ▷ ⬚ ⬚

However, the swing of the limbs (in this case the right arm) follows a more complicated trace-form. Radiating paths, leading from the centre to the periphery of the kinesphere, or vice versa, have to be distinguished from curving paths which go around the centre, along the boundary of the kinesphere.

The following outline indicates the approximate path or track of the whole defence sequence. The outline is simplified and related to the dimensional directions only. In reality, the movement follows more complicated paths.

As stated above, the movement of the "prime" leads to high, ⬚. Beginning at the point forward, ⬚, where the "sixth" was terminated, the direct path from ⬚ to ⬚ deviates towards the centre, ⬚, of both body and kinesphere owing to the swinging action of the arm. Thus an arc is created via the centre which may be called a "central arc":

from ⬚ via ⬚ to ⬚

Continuing from there, the "second" leads to deep, ▮, and the path is deviated towards the periphery on the right side, ▷, thus forming a "peripheral arc":

from ⬚ via ▷ to ▮

Note that we call these arcs "deviations," which means that the intended path for some reason deviates towards a point of the kinesphere.

4

The "third" deviates towards the centre, and forms another "central arc":

from ▌ via ▯ to ◁

The "fourth" deviates towards forward and forms another "peripheral arc":

from ◁ via ▯ to ▷

The "fifth" deviates towards the centre, and forms a third "central arc":

from ▷ via ▯ to ▯

The "sixth" deviates towards deep, forming a third "peripheral arc":

from ▯ via ▮ to ▯

The whole line will read as indicated in Fig. 14, which shows the approximate track of the defence sequence which travels along curved paths formed

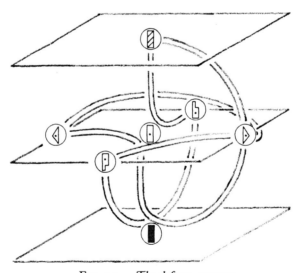

FIG. 14.—*The defence sequence.*

▯ ... (▯ ...) ▨ ... (▷ ...) ▮ ... (▯ ...)
◁ ... (▯ ...) ▷ ... (▯ ...) ▯ ... (▮ ...) |▯

(NOTE: the deviation points are put into parenthesis.)

by the deviating influence of spatial points. Similar deviations can be observed in the attacking movements.

A peculiarity of radiating movements should be mentioned. In general, they go to the periphery of the kinesphere within normal reach, but the radiation can also be restricted, or augmented. We can understand these different degrees of extension as taking place in a smaller or larger kinesphere. The possible nuances are, again, infinite. In practical choreutics, it suffices to have,

   1. A sign for spatial restriction. This is:

X (narrow)

and means that the movement takes place in a smaller kinesphere.

   2. A sign for spatial augmentation. This is:

Ͷ (wide)

and means that the movement takes place in a larger kinesphere than the normal one. We call the two signs indicating different degrees of spatial extension: "space measurement" signs.*

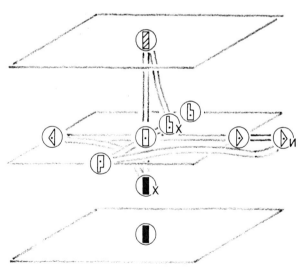

FIG. 15.—*Trace-form containing restricted and augmented radiations.*

* For further details about this the reader is referred to *Handbook of Kinetography Laban* by Albrecht Knust published by Macdonald & Evans.

Fig. 15 shows an example of a trace-form containing restricted and augmented radiations. In this trace-form, the signs "X" and "И" placed next to the directional symbols mean that the second and sixth movements in the sequence are executed very near the body, in a reduced kinesphere, while the fourth leads far away from it to the right, thus augmenting the kinesphere.

The conception of a shrinking and growing kinesphere in addition to the normal one makes it possible to describe innumerable variations of trace-forms.

The defence-scale takes on a slightly altered expression when the fundamental directions are replaced by primary deflected ones (*see* Chapter I). For example:

often shows the following form:

which is a deflected variation of the natural defence-scale.

Another different expression is given if the directions of the sequence are transformed into pure diagonals, although the general character of the sequence—here the defence character—remains. We have the following form:

The pure diagonal nature of this latter version gives it a more flowing expression and makes it less useful for practical defence. It has become a more dance-like variation of the fighting sequence.

Sequences in which the various kinds of deflection are mixed give numerous differentiations in the paths of movement. The following is a further variation of the defence scale:

Note that the steps employed in fencing always lead approximately forwards, ♮, or backwards, ♭. When fighting is performed as a kind of dance-play, it is, of course, quite possible to execute any steps or gestures with the legs accompanying the arm movements. The extremely important question of how the limbs function in relation to one another will be dealt with in the next chapter.

Fighting might be classified as a quite general form of movement. One might almost say that all our everyday activities, especially those when working, are a form of fighting; a struggle with objects, with material, with tools. In addition, however, there is an entirely different kind of motion, namely locomotion, which is the process of moving to a new place in the general space by walking, running, jumping, swimming, or some similar action.

When we study the action of swimming, we note that there are numerous ways of moving through the water. The most usual of these are the breast-stroke and the crawl. Each of these two methods requires a different use of the body. In the breast-stroke the movement of the body is symmetrical while in the crawl there are asymmetric body tensions because the right and left sides alternate. In both cases the movements follow a definite series of spatial directions, which can be analysed according to the principles already mentioned.

Fig. 16 shows the trace-form of a "crawl-like" movement of both arms in an upright position. When propelling oneself through water with a crawl-stroke each arm performs a winding loop similar to that illustrated, one arm starting with the other following after a period of time as in a musical canon. When the first arm has completed half the loop, the second begins its corresponding part. The legs make only small movements, rather like steps, changing between forward and backward, but the flexible movements of the upper part of the torso assist with the shaping of the trace-form.

Now we come to the question of why in the crawl-stroke this particular sequence of spatial directions is followed, and not another. The canon-like series of movements is not a solo effort of one side of the body only, as in fencing, but a duet between the two. In fencing, each movement was determined by the needs of defence or attack. Its sequence had a definite and purposive form, from the first movement to the sixth and last. Here also, the determining factor of this special arrangement is the purpose of the

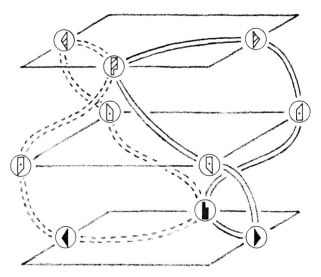

FIG. 16.—*Trace-form of "crawl-like" movement.*

Right arm:
Left arm:

movement, which is to overcome the resistance of the water with the greatest economy of effort. This requires adaptation of the movements to the structure of the body which is bound up, as we have seen, with the harmonic laws of space, and with the fluidity of the surrounding element.

The movement itself is fluid and much more mobile than in fencing, where the firm foothold makes it seem relatively static. This is not the only difference between movements in fencing and in swimming. The movements of the crawl-stroke are essentially peripheral, reaching out to the periphery of the kinesphere with the muscular force exerted from the extremities, whereas in fencing the movements tend to be centralised and the force concentrated around the centre of the kinesphere, in attacking or defending its kernel, the body.

In comparing the zones of the limbs (*see* Chapter II) which are utilised in the two activities just investigated, we can see that in fencing the dimensional directions prevail, while the loops of the crawl-stroke tend towards more diagonally located areas.

The two contrasting fundamentals on which all choreutic harmony is based are the dimensional tension and the diagonal tension. Basic sequences can be built up on these two principles. Such scales, being based on natural movement which corresponds to the structure of the body, may be called "natural sequences" in space.

In performing movements similar to the crawl-stroke with a trace-form of a winding loop, we come close to the various swinging movements which appear in dance. They can lead into various places of the normal, the restricted and the augmented kinesphere, and follow a great variety of directions.

Fourth fact of space-movement

It is natural for all living organisms to use the simplest and easiest paths in space when fighting, not only when the fight is a matter of life and death, but also in other activities, since all working is a kind of fighting and struggling with objects and materials. Everywhere economy of effort is in evidence, including all kinds of bodily locomotion.

In the art of movement, and particularly in dance, economy of effort is coupled either with an emphasised play of keeping or giving up equilibrium, or with a refined employment of harmonious combinations of the same dynamic patterns that occur in everyday movement.

CHAPTER V

The Body and Trace-forms

WHEN we lift one arm from its hanging position at our side, we trace a form resembling the shape of an opening fan. Our shoulder is the handle of the fan, and the hand describes the line of the outer semicircle. It is the same with movements of the legs if they are lifted straight up into any direction in space. The trunk can also make such fan-like movements, for instance in bending forward. The difference between the opening of a fan and the movement of the human limb is that the series of the opening ribs of the fan are still visible as the movement is completed, while the arm or leg in its final position is, for our eyes, the only remaining part of the movement.

In observing a movement we must visualise all the intermediary stages of its unfolding. In describing movement, we must make a mental note of the most important intermediary positions. This is the procedure we have already employed in former chapters, when analysing and describing the movements of fencing, and so on. It is also possible to make three-dimensional or plastic models which retain each stage of the unfolding of the movement. We sometimes see such forms in skirt-dancing, or when an arm, clothed in a wide sleeve, is lifted. These formations, like a bat's wing, follow not only flat planes but sometimes very complicated curved surfaces and serpentine forms. All bending and stretching movements of any part of the limbs, for instance of the fore-arms, or the lower part of the legs, the hands, or the head (an extension of the spinal column), always trace such fan-like patterns.

When we create a cone-shaped trace-form with one of our limbs, it suffices to note only three or four ribs, or spokes, of the shape. Normally, the movement will be executed smoothly in a continuous curve. If we wish to perform angular sections, we must give each section a special accentuation.

Fig. 17 illustrates a cone-shaped trace-form following the directions ♮, ♮,

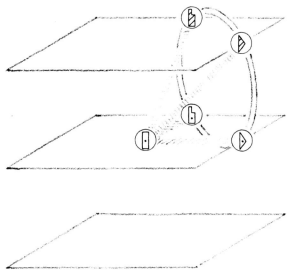

FIG. 17.—*Cone-shaped trace-form smoothly rounded.*

♭, ♭, and again ♮ , executed smoothly in a continuously curving pattern. The same trace-form when executed in a broken or angular way, with almost imperceptible pauses between each section, is shown in Fig. 18.

The complex feeling we have when seeing or executing a movement cannot be described in words. It is, however, possible to analyse the essential

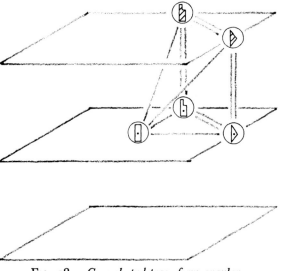

FIG. 18.—*Cone-shaped trace-form angular.*

volition inherent in each movement. The best way is to separate the patterns of lines and forms which the moving body traces in space from the other components of the movement. The action of the whole body or different parts of it seems to be set off by the will to move. Each step and gesture calls for a series of contractions and extensions in the muscles themselves and also the transference of the body, or its limbs, from one place to another. All these activities need both space and time. However, they are generally prompted by a thought or an intention which may be a purely practical one, such as the desire to make a change in our circumstances or surroundings. We call this "action," using the word in a particular sense, for in the broader sense, even the changing of weight or the play of the muscles is, in reality, an action. We cannot even be sure whether the decision to move is an action of which we can become aware and which we can control, but in any case each movement has, apart from creating a new situation in both time and space, other inherent qualities.

The will or the decision to move springs from the depth of our being. We not only alter the positions of our bodies and change the environment by our activity, but bring an additional colour or mood to our movements from our psyche. We speak of feeling, or thought which precedes or accompanies movements.

An observer of a moving person is at once aware, not only of the paths and rhythms of movement, but also of the mood the paths in themselves carry, because the shapes of the movements through space are always more or less coloured by a feeling or an idea. The content of ideas and feelings which we have when moving or seeing movement can be analysed as well as the forms and lines in space. One can use for this purpose the language of psychology and philosophy.

In general, lines and forms can easily be understood and described using the terminology of mathematics and geometry. Choreutics has a special way with its own language and script (choreology and choreography) of analysing and defining movements. It is the basis of a notation not only of dances but of movement in general. When we look at signs stemming from ancient civilisations, such as from Chinese, Indian, Celtic, Germanic and Aztecan cultures, it seems that a kind of choreutic symbol writing, now practically forgotten, was widely employed in those times.

To separate bodily functions (meaning anatomical and physiological) from spatial activity (meaning that which creates the shapes and lines in space) is in reality as impossible as to separate the mental and emotional parts of movement from the space forms in which they become visible. It is certain, however, that not only the spectator but also the moving person often recognises the emotional content of a movement only after it has been completed. A completely voluntary movement, in which every detail is premeditated and controlled, is for the dancer or the actor a very rare fulfilment. The true artist at least approaches this perfection, while the average man is often far from it, or indeed from any conscious expression whatever. He fails in the form, or in the mood, or in most cases in both. It is interesting to note, however, that people with excessively controlled movement, like bad actors, fail to communicate their intended response, and we cannot help but doubt the sincerity of their actions. Only when a part of the quality of movement is, or seems to be, unconscious do we speak of a natural or true expression.

From the choreutic point of view, it is not necessary to denote in every case which limb is employed to execute a particular trace-form. A trace-form supplies a certain inspiration as does a melody; the details of the execution of it by the body can often be left to the individual taste of the performer. There are, nevertheless, the natural zones of the different limbs (as mentioned in Chapter II), which should be taken into consideration.

When following a trace-form, whether with a single limb or several limbs together, we produce all the well-known actions of grasping, jumping, turning and also the various positions of kneeling, lying, standing and sitting. All these actions can be expressed by spatial signs, and may be distinguished either as polylinear movements (several limbs, or parts of a limb, moving simultaneously into different directions) or as monolinear movements (one limb, or part of a limb, moving into one direction at any one time).

When speaking of the body and trace-forms, we must examine the particular functions of the limbs. The most apparent activities are for the arms, gathering and scattering movements, and for the legs, taking steps. All these as well as the movements of the legs preparatory to stepping take place in the zones associated with the limbs concerned. Gathering or taking is usually associated with a turning of the palms towards the body. In the contrary movement, scattering, or rejecting, an outward turning of the palms is generally used.

The zones can be outlined with the palms of the hands turned either outward or inward. The position assumed need not be limited by hard-and-fast
rules, because it depends solely on the purpose of the movement. This may
be strictly utilitarian, as when grasping an object, or could act as a purely
artistic gesture, when the scope of the movement would depend on the
demands of the idea to be expressed. Individual styles, although in an art
form of utmost importance, should never become standardised rules for
general use.

The body has a feeling of contraction in gathering, whilst the opposite,
scattering, gives a feeling of opening out and of expansion. When the trunk
or the shoulders participate, the movement becomes more complex; the
various parts of the body may combine to create a single trace-form, or they
may produce differing trace-forms. The outlines of these forms are always
curved, since movements of the limbs or other parts of the body are conditioned by their joint attachments. The curves can be followed along the
circumference of the kinesphere in a clockwise or a counter-clockwise direction. These directions of circling are related to a directional ray of the
kinesphere which serves as an axis.

We therefore have the following basic possibilities which are illustrated
in Figs. 19a–f:

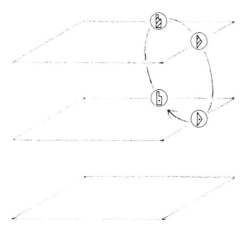

Fig. 19a.—*Following a single trace-form clockwise.*

1. Following a single trace-form clockwise (Fig. 19*a*).
2. Following the same trace-form counter-clockwise (Fig. 19*b*).
3. Following different trace-forms clockwise (Fig. 19*c*).

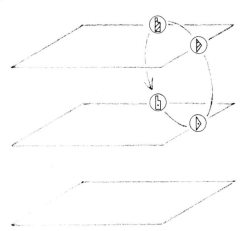

FIG. 19*b*.—*Following the same trace-form counter-clockwise.*

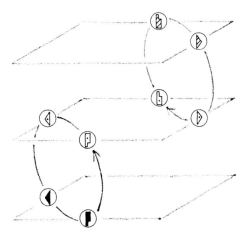

FIG. 19*c*.—*Following different trace-forms clockwise.*

4. Following the same trace-forms counter-clockwise (Fig. 19*d*).
5. Following a single trace-form first counter-clockwise and then clock-wise (Fig. 19*e*).
6. Following different trace-forms partly clockwise, partly counter-clock-wise (Fig. 19*f*).

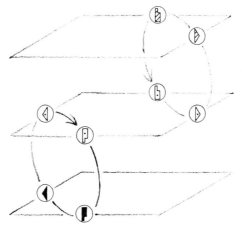

FIG. 19*d*.—*Following the same trace-forms counter-clockwise.*

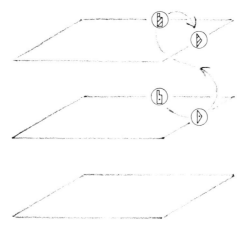

FIG. 19*e*.—*Following a single trace-form first counter-clockwise and then clockwise.*

starts counter-clockwise
and continues clockwise

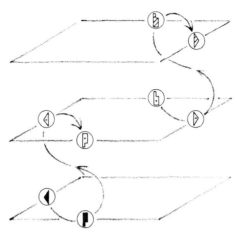

Fig. 19f.—*Following different trace-forms partly clock-wise, partly counter-clockwise. In each case the movement is viewed from the centre of the kinesphere.*

starts counter-clockwise and continues clockwise

starts clockwise and continues counter-clockwise

We must keep in mind, as stated in Chapter II, that the limbs have super-zones as well as normal zones, which means that they can pass into neighbouring zones as well. Trace-forms are not tied to any one bodily zone, but can evolve within a large number of neighbouring zones.

Trace-forms and bodily attitudes both seem to have an independent life of their own. A trace-form for the right arm, for instance:

which would normally be executed as a gathering movement, could be performed with the palms turned outward as in scattering. This independence, however, is not a reality. (The possible errors in both perceiving and analysing movement are described in Chapter VIII.)

The particular way of using a limb, which is determined by an outer need of action or an inner need of expression, creates a secondary trace-form, which unfolds within the muscles of the body. This muscular trace-form and the gesture-line in space together form a kind of counterpoint. The secondary trace-form might be compared with the accompanying figures in music and the other with its melodic line.

The movements of the limbs as they evolve in the kinesphere must be distinguished from the actions in the dynamosphere. Though they always appear together, it is within the body that dynamic actions such as wringing, pressing, etc., occur (*see* Chapter III).

Dynamospheric as well as kinespheric actions are located somewhere in space, and are composed of directional tendencies and polarities. An electromagnetic current is said to be the physical agent of the irritation which causes the intention, decision, and finally the action itself. We believe that the cause of the irritation is, in general, an outside impression to which we react by making the decision to move. Both the actual or remembered impression is again a spatial occurrence.

The first impulse of such a series of impressions and reactions lies in infinitely remote time and space, and is completely uncontrollable. The role which the future plays in this chain of happenings becomes comprehensible through the fact that each movement tends to create a new situation. Each bodily action is only a step towards an infinitely remote last goal in future time-space, which for our minds is as intangible and uncontrollable as the first cause.

Fifth fact of space-movement

Each bodily movement is embedded in a chain of infinite happenings from which we distinguish only the immediate preceding steps and, occasionally, those which immediately follow.

In every trace-form, created by the body, both infinity and eternity are hidden. Sometimes the veil seems to be lifted for an instant. Inspiration, clairvoyance, and a heightened awareness can thrive from this fissure in the part of the world which we see as eternity. Thus bodily actions and trace-forms become a means of producing moments of ecstasy or clairvoyant concentration. We should never forget that every gesture and action of our body is a deeply rooted mystery and not a mere outward function or trick, as many people regard it in modern times. It was thus that tumbling or standing on the head could once have been a sacred play.

CHAPTER VI

Natural Sequences of the Dynamosphere

THE natural sequences of the dynamosphere consist of chains of dynamic actions, with their corresponding inner moods. As they are of a purely expressive nature, originating from within the person and containing mental and emotional qualities, we might indeed refer to them as "action-moods." We are not completely free to connect the eight actions mentioned in Chapter III in any way we may desire. The transition from a pressing movement to a wringing movement, for instance, can be easily performed without a perceptible break, but it is impossible to make an equally smooth transition from a pressing to a slashing movement. However, the transition from wringing to slashing, or vice versa, is easily done. Thus we see that there are certain action-moods which are closely related to each other, and that some are loosely linked, whilst others are diametrically opposed.

It is one of the most striking discoveries in the domain of choreutics that an oddness and an affinity exist between action-moods, and that this relationship can be expressed by space symbols. The diagonal directions which characterise related action-moods lie closer to one another in space than those of the action-moods which cannot be so easily connected.

A remarkable fact is that there is a close proximity in kinespheric space between related action-moods, and a growing distance between action-moods of estranged inner relations. The eight fundamental dynamic actions are composed of three basic dynamic traits: speed, force and directional flux.

These dynamic traits have different degrees of intensity, leading to two contrasting elements within each. Rapidity is a higher degree of speed than slowness. Strength is a higher degree of force than weakness. Straightness is a higher degree of directional flux than roundaboutness.

The actions are characterised by the intensity-degree of the dynamic traits they contain. For instance, when a right-side limb leads:

◣s (pressing) consists of ◳s (slow) ■s (strong) ◁s (straight)
◤s (wringing) consists of ◳s (slow) ■s (strong) ◌s (roundabout)

Pressing and wringing have the same speed, ◳s , and the same strength, ■s , but they differ in their degree of directional flux; while ◣s (pressing) is straight ◁s , ◤s (wringing) is ◌s roundabout.

Thus we can say that pressing differs from wringing in the degree of one of the basic traits, namely that of directional flux, where the element of straightness is replaced by that of roundaboutness.

There are actions which have only one element in common, therefore they differ in two aspects. Those differing in all three elements are complete contrasts.

Experience proves that extreme contrasts of dynamic actions in which there are contrasting elements of all three fundamental traits, speed, force and directional flux, cannot be performed by the body immediately one after the other. Transitional movements must be introduced. For instance:

Linking a punching movement ▮s with a floating movement ◿s without a break is quite impossible, and therefore two transitory movements must be inserted. Punching ▮s , when performed by a right-side limb consists of:

◗s (quick), ◁s (straight), ■s (strong).

However, when the speed is changed from ◗s (quick) to ◳s (slow), we have:

◳s (slow), ◁s (straight), ■s (strong),

which is pressing ◣s , a first intermediary step towards the floating movement to which we wish to change.

Changing now the degree of another trait, for instance that of directional flux, we have again a different kind of action:

◳s (slow), ◌s (roundabout), ■s (strong),

which is wringing ◤s , a second intermediary stage, differing from the original punching in two elements. It now differs from floating, to which we wish to change the movement, in the degree of only one dynamic trait: force.

Changing the degree of intensity of force, the third dynamic trait, from $\blacksquare_s$ (strong) to $\emptyset_s$ (light) produces:

$$\flat_s \text{ (slow)}, \quad \triangleright_s \text{ (roundabout)}, \quad \emptyset_s \text{ (light)},$$

which is floating $\emptyset_s$. Thus the original punching movement $\blacktriangledown_s$ has been linked with the opposing floating movement $\emptyset_s$ by means of the intermediary stages $\blacktriangleright_s$ (pressing) and $\blacktriangleleft_s$ (wringing).

The succession of such intermediary actions between complete contrasts may be referred to as natural sequences in the dynamosphere. All actions can be linked together by a series of intermediary movements. Between one action-mood and its extreme contrast there are six possible series of connection. For instance, Fig. 20 shows the natural sequence in the

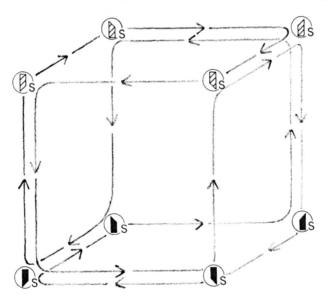

FIG. 20.—*Natural sequence in the dynamosphere— between punching and floating.*

$$\blacktriangledown_s | \cdots (\flat_s \cdots \emptyset_s \cdots) \emptyset_s | \cdots (\emptyset_s \cdots \flat_s \cdots) \blacktriangledown_s |$$
$$\blacktriangledown_s | \cdots (\blacktriangleleft_s \cdots \emptyset_s \cdots) \emptyset_s | \cdots (\blacktriangleleft_s \cdots \blacktriangleright_s \cdots) \blacktriangledown_s |$$
$$\blacktriangledown_s | \cdots (\blacktriangleright_s \cdots \blacktriangleleft_s \cdots) \emptyset_s | \cdots (\emptyset_s \cdots \blacktriangleright_s \cdots) \blacktriangledown_s |$$

(Note: the intermediary movements are in parentheses.)

dynamosphere between the contrasting action-moods, ▮ₛ(punching) and ▱ₛ (floating).

The linking of any action-moods produces a kind of trace-form which does not always take on a definite kinespheric shape but influences the dynamic expression of the move. This might be looked upon as a "shadow-form," which connects the centralised living energy with actions in kinespheric space. An example of this is given in Fig. 21 which shows three diagonals as axes for shadow-forms.

In contrast to Fig. 21, Fig. 22 shows one loop of the shadow-form of a natural sequence between two contrasting action-moods. Here it is fully developed in kinespheric space.

The three other pairs of action-moods of which each single part is in extreme contrast to its partner are:

◣ₛ (slashing)   ◿ₛ (gliding)
◤ₛ (wringing)   ◺ₛ (dabbing)
◥ₛ (pressing)   ◹ₛ (flicking)

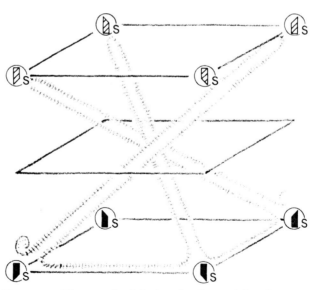

FIG. 21.—*Diagram of a "shadow-form" containing three axes.*

| ▮ₛ ··· ◿ₛ ··· ▮ₛ ··· ◣ₛ ··· ◺ₛ ··· ◣ₛ ··· ◤ₛ ··· ◺ₛ ··· ◤ₛ |

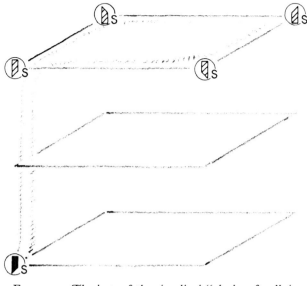

FIG. 22.—*The loop of the visualised "shadow-form" in the natural sequence.*

They have similar series of connection to those in Fig. 20. In these sequences are found all natural links which arise in the bodily execution of simple dynamic action-moods.

As indicated in Chapter III, further relations such as those of deflected directions can be developed in the dynamosphere. Just as the deflected directions consist of only two components so do also their dynamospheric counterparts. In linking one with another, for instance: $\natural_s$ (light/slow) with $\flat_s$ (light/roundabout), the change involved is one of kind and not of degree, i.e. from a degree of speed to one of directional flux, while that of force remains constant. In this case the transitory movements which link the natural sequences are either omitted, or minimised to such an extent that they become almost imperceptible.

Such combinations, not included in the natural sequences, can be regarded as variations and mixtures. Man has complete freedom in his choice and employment of action-moods. Yet he is unable to connect directly, without a more or less perceptible transition, two of the action-moods which are not close neighbours in the natural sequences.

The first movement ⌀ ... ▌ in the above analysis of the "twisted, concentrated attitude in angry preparation for aggression" travels along the diagonal axis. It represents the action-moods ⌀ₛ... ▌ₛ, between which is the greatest possible degree of distance in the dynamosphere.

We know that there are six ways, each leading along two intermediary links, from contrast to contrast. Three of them are situated in the region of the normal zones for the limbs on the right side, and three for the limbs on the left. If we take the right side to be the active one, the following scheme gives us an example of right side "natural" ways:

$$⌀ₛ \cdots ◣ₛ \cdots ◣ₛ \cdots ▌ₛ$$
$$⌀ₛ \cdots ⌀ₛ \cdots ◣ₛ \cdots ▌ₛ$$
$$⌀ₛ \cdots ◪ₛ \cdots ⌀ₛ \cdots ▌ₛ$$

The second way:

$$⌀ₛ \cdots ⌀ₛ \cdots ◣ₛ \cdots ◣ₛ$$

would appear to be the most balanced one.

Performing this line in the kinesphere:

$$⌀ \cdots ⌀ \cdots ◣ \cdots ▌$$

with the corresponding expression, we realise that it is the most typical movement for the aforementioned emotional action: "twisted, concentrated attitude in angry preparation for aggression."

As often mentioned, words have only an explanatory value in choreutics. With the help of our symbols we are able to state more simply that a harmonious flow of emotions exists. We are even able to construct a kind of dynamic standard scale, in which a chain of harmoniously linked emotions is related to a kinespheric trace-form of the same shape. Such a chain is shown in Fig. 23.

(NOTE: the action-moods in parentheses do not lead to diagonals but to deflected inclinations. Their expression is also not a pure one in the sense of the eight basic action-moods, but is a less complete one.)

This sequence of action-moods can be approximately explained in words.

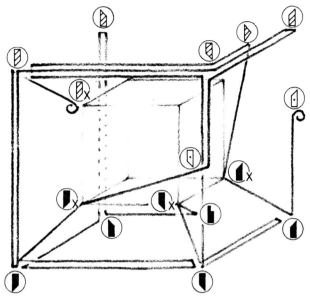

FIG. 23.—*Chain of inner attitudes as visualised in kinespheric space.*

If the dynamospheric line is transferred into the kinesphere, and the intermediary links between opposing action-moods are accentuated, the changes between these (performing with the right side) could be explained thus:

lively enthusiastic gesture preceding a reaching up with calm detachment,

agitated move changing into concentrated position as if in preparation for angry attack, abrupt turn, as if fleeing from danger, leading to a gesture of guarded cautiousness,

$$\text{\ding{}}_s \cdots \text{\ding{}}_s \cdots (\text{\ding{}}_s) \cdots \text{\ding{}}_{sx} \cdots \text{\ding{}}_s$$

determined move in preparation for a gesture of proud defiance,

$$\text{\ding{}}_s \cdots \text{\ding{}}_s \cdots \text{\ding{}}_s \cdots \text{\ding{}}_s$$

brusque recoil and trembling, as if with shock, coming to a petrified stop,

$$\text{\ding{}}_s \cdots \text{\ding{}}_s \cdots (\text{\ding{}}_s) \cdots \text{\ding{}}_{sx} \cdots \text{\ding{}}_s \cdots \mid (\text{\ding{}}_s)$$

effusive gesture of intense feeling, as if approaching a person or situation with sympathy, ending in a relaxed manner.

Replacing the transitory stages (action-moods) of this line by the dimensional tendency contained in each section, thus:

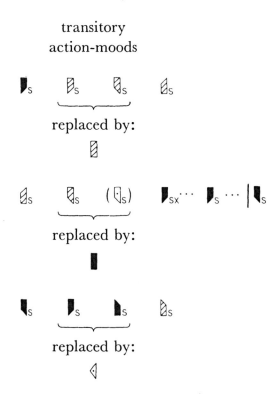

transitory
action-moods

transitory
action-moods

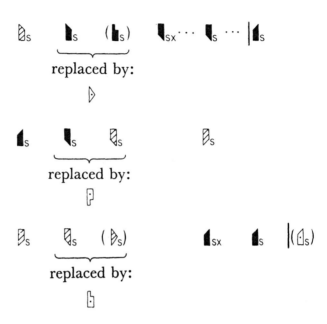

we arrive at the dimensional scheme of the defence-scale with a secondary (shadow) line, indicating an appropriate dynamic expression:

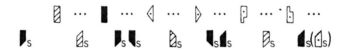

Almost any kinespheric trace-form can be accompanied by any dynamospheric sequence. Some combinations will be more appropriate, while others will appear almost completely incompatible. Variations of a natural sequence in the kinesphere can be accompanied by one and the same shadow-form in the dynamosphere; variations of the dynamosphere can be accompanied by one and the same trace-form in the kinesphere. That is to say, the dynamospheric influence of an action-mood or a shadow-form (series of action-moods) can be felt anywhere, in any direction of the kinesphere. Yet it is quite possible for the kinespheric evolutions to coincide with their dynamospheric equivalents. In such a case we may speak of the transference of the dynamospheric shadow-form into the kinesphere, or vice versa as already mentioned.

Sixth fact of space-movement

The manifestations of our inner being become evident in almost invisible shadow-forms, giving more emotional colour than spatial form. These often occur in very small expressive movements of the face, hands and other parts of the body. They have, nevertheless, a spatial architecture, which can be both controlled and investigated. Being motions, the sequences of emotions have a perceptible flow in which certain harmonic unfoldings can be noticed. These almost invisible shadow-forms can be compared with the almost inaudible overtones in music.

When a tone sounds, a series of sympathetic vibrations occur which are audible as very soft overtones. The first one to be perceived is the octave which is followed by a number of other overtones. Many of them can be clearly distinguished, while an endless suite of every imaginable nuance gradually becomes softer and softer until they are no longer perceptible to the ear.

When we perform a movement a similar thing happens. It seems, however, that the succession of what we perceive happens in reverse. While in music the tone and its octave appear first and then the other nuances, the first things we perceive in movement are the fine nuances of the shadow-forms, and only when the emotional tone or action-mood is determined does the real trace-form become visible in the kinesphere.

The influence which a shadow-form has on a trace-form can be established by analysing and experiencing the structure of a trace-form. Shadow-forms demand a response from our whole personality, when their structure-line is made clear and performed fluently. Both impulse and response appear to be more easily felt by a person who has a certain gift for moving expressively. However, almost anyone can develop a certain degree of awareness of the connection between motion and emotion through appropriate exercises. The expression will always be more or less personal, but the fundamental responses, given by different people to the same impulse, all seem to have some typical characteristics, based on the harmonic laws which rule all movements in space.

The tradition of creating and recording artistic movement in dancing and miming might assist us to clarify the relationship between dynamospheric and kinespheric sequences. The order which may be said to exist between the various action-moods, as well as in the shadow-forms resulting from them, can be expressed in terms of spatial harmony. A law of proximity can be perceived; proximity of action-moods makes shadow-forms more related, while distance makes them lack relatedness. A bodily feeling for harmonious movement does not permit immediate transition between distant action-moods in the dynamosphere. The order can also be expressed by an approximate description of the emotional character of movements which are connected with a definite shadow-form.

We are only at the beginning of a deeper awareness of this whole field and its importance. So far the experience of the interdependence of dynamo-spheric and kinespheric sequences has shown us that the conventional idea of space as a phenomenon which can be separated from time and force and from expression, is completely erroneous.

CHAPTER VII

The Standard Scale

IT now becomes necessary to give further attention to the structure of the kinespheric "scaffolding." This is characterised by two main types of tensions:

    1. Between the surface-lines or edges.

    2. Between the lines traversing the scaffolding—the dimensions, the diagonals, the diameters and the "transversals." The latter distinguish themselves by not intersecting at the centre of the kinesphere, while all the others do (*see* Chapter I). They lie between three diagonals or three dimensionals, or more precisely athwart them and, therefore, do not form a plane with any two. We consider them to be "secondary deflections" from the diagonals and dimensionals. They always connect two end-points of two different diameters. They never link endpoints of dimensionals or diagonals, or form a surface-line of the scaffolding.

The scaffolding of the kinesphere built up so far has 24 surface-lines which are parallel to the six primary deflected inclinations, which we call diameters. Each diameter has four parallel surface-lines. For instance:

diameter ◖ ◗ is parallel to

◖ ··· ◗, ◖ ··· ◗, ◖ ··· ◗; ◖ ··· ◗

Each diagonal is surrounded by a chain of six transversals (a "cluster"), a chain of six surface-lines (a "girdle") and two "polar triangles," each of which joins by surface-lines the extremities of the transversals forming the cluster.

As an example we may take the diagonal ◖ ... ◗ . This is associated with the cluster which is illustrated in Fig. 24. The same diagonal is surrounded

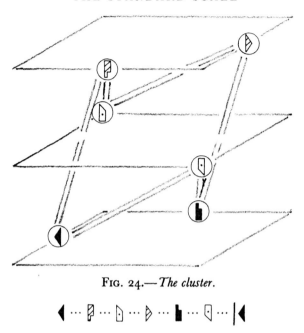

FIG. 24.—*The cluster.*

by the girdle as shown in Fig. 25 and by the two polar triangles which are

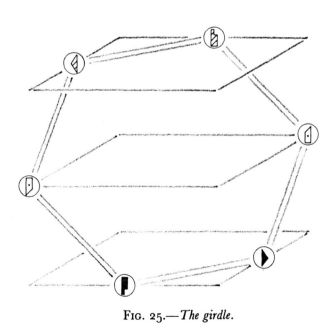

FIG. 25.—*The girdle.*

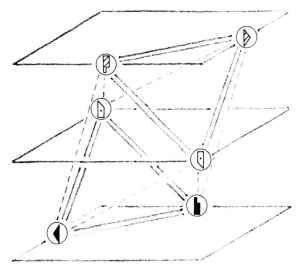

FIG. 26.—*The two polar triangles*

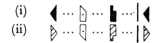

illustrated in Fig. 26, where the broken lines represent the transversals of the cluster which connect the two triangles.

A diagonal which is the axis of a cluster of six transversals is comparable to the axis of the earth, while the girdle of six surface-lines corresponds to the equator.

(NOTE: it should be mentioned that as the earth rotates on its axis, this tilted axis moves around in a circle forming a double conical trace-line. We can understand the two polar triangles mentioned above as the line along which the axis of the cluster makes similar revolving movements.)

We can follow both the cluster and the girdle with our movements. Movements which follow the chain of the cluster are seen in nature among animals in captivity, or, in the swaying of a drunken man, or one who is tired or falling asleep. It is, in general, an unconscious and involuntary movement.

Movements which follow the chain of the girdle are seen in nature in emphatic gestures and actions. They are, in general, voluntary movements. The emphasis contains, however, a certain state of unconscious excitement, but this excitement is a kind of day-dream. Man is awake in the equatorial, and not asleep as in the axial cluster movements.

The hybrid offspring of these two contrasting kinds of movement, the automatic, sleep-like one, and the inspired wakeful one, is a third mode of movement which is more difficult to describe in a single word than the two others. In this mode man follows a series of intermediary chains of trace-forms which, like an electrical discharge, strike from the cluster to the girdle, and vice versa. In our ordinary everyday working movements and general locomotion we employ these intermediary chains of trace-forms, sometimes falling into automatic movement, and at others into emphatic movement. In dancing and fighting man has a tendency mainly to use emphatic movement. This is also the case in emotional outbursts which are often characterised by uncontrolled jumps from the emphatic to the automatic, leaving out that mode of movement which is apparent in ordinary everyday working actions and general locomotion. In other words, in cases of emotional outburst, we use cluster and girdle trace-forms in turn without intermediary links.

These links form the third mode of movement which becomes evident in a simple surface-line connecting the cluster with the girdle. It starts from

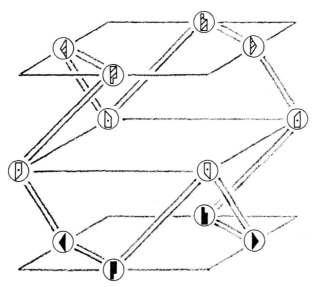

FIG. 27.—*Chain of twelve surface-lines—peripheral standard scale—revolving around axis:*

one point on the girdle and travels to the next on the cluster, and so on alternately, until the circuit is completed. The circuit touches twelve points. Fig. 27 is an example in which the chain revolves around the diagonal axis ▌ ... �“ .

When we examine the chain the following picture arises:

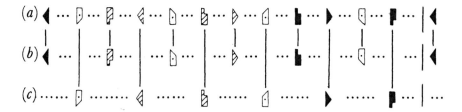

The first sequence (*a*) represents the complete chain. The second sequence (*b*) indicates the points of the cluster extracted from the chain, and the third sequence (*c*) shows the points of the girdle also extracted from the chain. It can therefore be seen that beginning, for instance, with ◀ which is a point of the cluster, each second step is again a point of the cluster, alternating with one of the girdle.

All this has a deeper meaning. The unconscious automation associated with the cluster is counterbalanced by the wakeful emphasis associated with the girdle. Therefore, movements which are neither automatic nor emphatic will follow trace-forms of a chain within the twelve-link chain, which is the prototype of all ordinary movement chains, and thus it may be considered as the "standard" scale.* This standard scale can revolve around various axes with different orientations, but its form remains the same. The inner cause of a change of axis is a change of mood or feeling, or of practical intention. For instance, the need or decision of attack or defence causes either an increase of mobility or an increase in stability. It may be recalled that series of other mental and emotional nuances are reflected in the particular orientation of the axis (*see* Chapters III and IV).

The standard scale is especially useful as it can be shown to contain a series of shapes which are the basic elements of almost all trace-forms employed in movement. Each chain of twelve links can be divided into six, four, three or two parts. The points of these divisions when joined together form regular polygons, that is, hexagons, quadrangles, and triangles, and in

* Also known as "primary" scale.

the case of two parts, a straight line. An uneven division of the chain would produce a series of irregular polygons.

These polygons, especially the regular ones, are related to the trace-forms of certain characteristic movements. As these shapes are traced by movement in three-dimensional space, they are not always geometrical forms in a plane. We find in practice that some of them form different plastic variations of themselves. For instance, when connecting each second point (that is dividing the standard scale into six parts and joining the points of division) we get, as we have seen before, the lines of the girdle and the cluster. They are both hexagons. The hexagon of the girdle lies in one plane. The chain of six links of the cluster forms a zigzag line in three-dimensional space and it is therefore a plastic variation of a hexagon.

The boundary lines of both the plane hexagon of the girdle and the plastic hexagon of the cluster each have relationships with the diagonal which they surround and with the three dimensions. To explain this relationship we might say that the inclinations of their boundaries can be expressed as a deflection of a diagonal by one of the three dimensions.

There are 24 transversals in the scaffolding. They represent twelve secondary deflected inclinations (*cf.* primary deflected inclinations in Chapter I), since two are always parallel to each other. The secondary deflections are inclined towards one of the dimensions, and at the same time towards one of the diagonals. The value of their deflections can be expressed as follows:

Dimensions:	Diagonals:	Transversals and their parallels or secondary deflections:	Corresponding diameters or primary deflections:

continued overleaf

Dimensions:	Diagonals:	Transversals and their parallels or secondary deflections:	Corresponding diameters or primary deflections:

(eight rows of Laban choreutic notation symbols)

A diagonal also can be deflected:

   (*a*) towards the vertical, meaning in the directions of a movement of the body stretching upwards or sinking downwards (height); such inclinations are called "steep";

   (*b*) towards the horizontal forward and backward, meaning the directions of the advancing or retreating of the body (depth); such inclinations are called "flowing";

   (*c*) towards the horizontal sideways, meaning in the directions of the opening or crossing of the arms (breadth); such inclinations are called "flat."

NOTE: "deflected diagonals" go through the centre of the kinesphere and the above-mentioned transversals are parallel to them, and therefore also have a steep, flowing or flat character.

When we follow the line of the cluster in a clockwise direction we find the same order of these three kinds of deflections. Starting with a vertical deflection, it follows a forward-backward deflection, and the last is a lateral deflection.

Example in the sequence of transversals in the cluster:

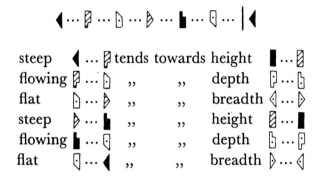

The inclinations of the surface-lines of the scaffolding which constitute the boundary lines of the girdle as shown in the following example:

follow the same order towards height, depth and breadth, as does the line of the cluster. They are, however, not transversals, but have the same inclinations as have diameters. In the scheme on pages 73 and 74, we showed the connections between transversal and diametral inclinations.

When connecting each third point (that is dividing the whole scale into four parts) the result is a quadrangle or square. The division may be undertaken from any point of the scale, for instance:

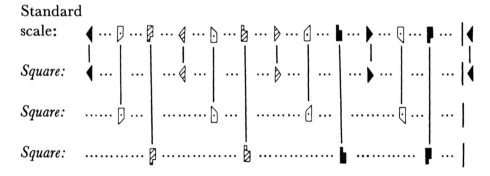

Similarly, when connecting each fourth point, which means dividing the whole scale into three parts, and joining the points of division, the result is a triangle, for instance:

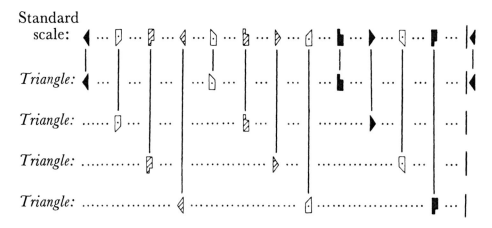

While the triangles lie in parallel planes, and are related to the girdle, the quadrangles intersect one another, build a plastic form, and are related to the cluster.

The relationship of the triangles to the girdle is of a separating nature: the planes and boundary lines of the triangles are parallel to the plane and boundary line of the girdle (*see* Fig. 28).

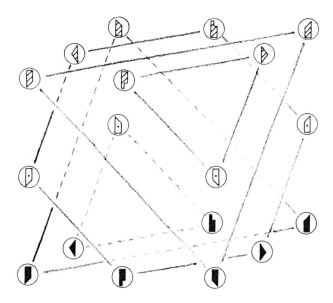

FIG. 28.—*Triangles and girdle.*

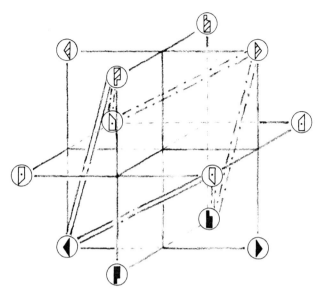

FIG. 29.—*Quadrangles and cluster.*

The relationship of the quadrangles to the cluster is of a connecting nature: the three quadrangles are bound together by the transversals of the cluster (*see* Fig. 29).

Dividing the standard scale into two parts, we get two points, whose connection forms a straight line, or diameter. There are, we must remember, six diameters in the scaffolding. Three diameters lie in the plane of the girdle, and the three others in a plastic (three-dimensional) situation across the cluster. Diameters in the girdle are:

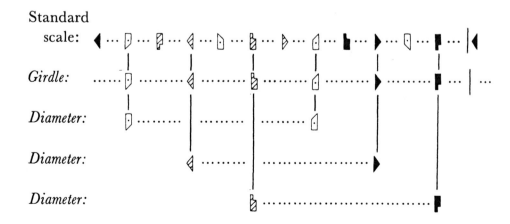

Diameters in the cluster are:

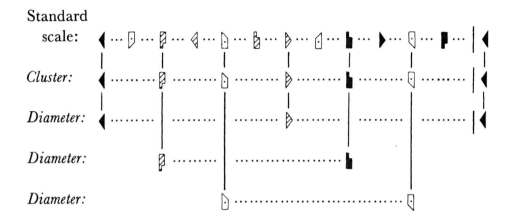

When we follow the clockwise flow of the standard scale, circling round several times and stopping at each fifth point, we get a twelve-link chain, built up by twelve transversals. This line is an inner counterpoint of the outer standard scale and, therefore, called the "transversal standard" scale.

An example of the inner counterpoint of the surface standard scale, connecting each fifth point of the latter is as follows:

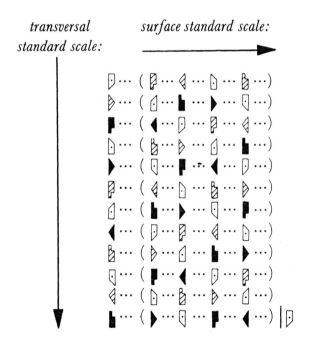

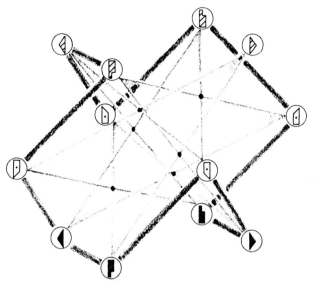

FIG. 30.—*Transversal standard scale revolving around axis:* ◙ ... ◗

In Fig. 30 the "inner" or "transversal" standard scale is represented.

A curious fact is that man understands his mirror-like symmetrical movements of left and right sides to be identical, although their inclinations are completely different. When someone follows with the right arm the trace-form of the outer standard scale around the axis:

and is asked to repeat the same movement with the left arm, he will not follow the same trace-form, but its mirrored form, a standard scale around the axis:

This feeling of uniformity in a mirror-like action is remarkable. It is interesting too that the two axes, around which the two trace-forms are felt to be identical, lie in a plane extending from left to right, inclined backward-upward:

Two other cubic axes exist in a left-right symmetrical plane, inclined forward-upward:

Around the two diagonals ♮ ... ▌ and ▐ ... ◹ lie outer standard scales which are felt as a kind of response to the one mentioned first. To explain the feeling of a response-form or echo-form, we must look at a peculiarity of the inner standard scale.

When performed with big looping swings the transversal standard scale has in its first half a similar expression to that of the defence scale in fighting (*see* Chapter IV).

> ⌐ ... ♭ is similar to a right-hand prime defence for the head.
> ♭ ... ▌ is similar to a 2nd defence for the right flank.
> ▐ ... ◠ is similar to a 3rd defence for the left upper side.
> ◡ ... ▸ is similar to a 4th defence for the right side.
> ▸ ... ◹ is similar to a 5th defence for the left flank.
> ◹ ... ◿ is similar to a 6th defence for the abdomen.

The transversal standard scale around the axis ♮ ... ▌ inclined forward-upward is felt as response- or echo-form to this and, instead of a series of defence movements, it contains a series of attack movements.

Let us suppose that the inclinations of our defence movements around our body can be fixed in space. If we turn half-way round, we find a scale which becomes an attack scale. This has remained in exactly the same place in the surrounding space, but through the turn it has changed its relation to the body.

If two people dance together, facing each other and holding right hands, one can execute the original transversal standard scale (defence character) and the other the echo standard scale (attack character) without letting go the hand of the other, so exact is the correspondence of the inclinations and the points reached in this kind of echo-like repetition. This may be considered as another form of symmetry.

A third kind of symmetry may be seen in the parallelism which exists in each inner standard scale itself, between its first and second half:

First half   *Second half*

◫ ... ◧ is parallel to ◩ ... ◀

◧ ··· ◼ ,,   ,,   ,,   ◀ ··· ◨

◼ ··· ◫ ,,   ,,   ,,   ◨ ··· ◪

◫ ··· ▶ ,,   ,,   ,,   ◪ ··· ◿

▶ ··· ◧ ,,   ,,   ,,   ◿ ··· ◼

◧ ··· ◩ ,,   ,,   ,,   ◼ ··· ◫

As shown above, in the second half of the scale the inclinations are parallel to those of the first half, but they are followed by the body in the contrary direction. Our intellect distinguishes between three forms of symmetry in space: up and down, left and right, forward and backward, but when the body follows trace-forms it appreciates only left-right symmetry. It would be interesting psychologically to investigate the causes and effects of this fact.

The surface or outer standard scale has forms similar to those of the transversal standard scale. There is the left-right version, the echo version, and the parallelism between the first and second half of each scale.

A surface standard scale consists of inclinations parallel to three of the six diameters:

◫ ... ◨ is parallel to the diameter ◀ ... ◧

◨ ··· ◧ ,,   ,,   ,,   ,,   ,,   ◫ ··· ◪

◧ ··· ◩ ,,   ,,   ,,   ,,   ,,   ◨ ··· ◼

◩ ··· ◼ ,,   ,,   ,,   ,,   ,,   ◧ ··· ◀

◼ ··· ▶ ,,   ,,   ,,   ,,   ,,   ◪ ··· ◫

▶ ··· ◪ ,,   ,,   ,,   ,,   ,,   ◼ ··· ◨

The three last diameters are the same as the three first, but in the reverse direction, since the second half of the surface standard scale is parallel to the first, but is performed in the reverse direction.

The body is aware of the wonderful order ruling the unfolding of trace-forms. This sense of harmony in space becomes visible and tangible in each movement. It is necessary to distinguish and understand the nuances of this feeling. As in music, a direct transmission of the harmonious feeling cannot be given in words, but can be achieved only by a sympathetic understanding of musical or choreutic symbols.

Seventh fact of space-movement

The twelve movements towards the twelve points of the kinesphere not only make a division of space possible, but also are in themselves units of harmonic interrelations. The criterion by which harmonic relations can be evaluated are the standard scales, which connect and accentuate the twelve points of the scaffolding. These could be called "signal-points."

In considering this, we can hope that the standard scales will become first an experiment, later an awareness of the curious structural world which forms the base of all impressions and expressions of our life.

CHAPTER VIII

Bodily Perspective

THE tradition of the dance enumerates four fundamental trace-forms which have the following shapes, called in the terminology of classical ballet:

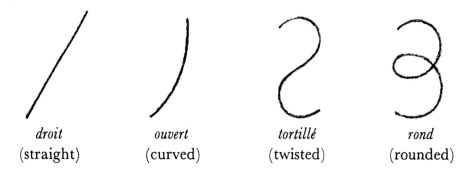

droit	*ouvert*	*tortillé*	*rond*
(straight)	(curved)	(twisted)	(rounded)

They are standard forms which recur in all human movements including those organised in scales, and they may evolve in space in one or several zones of the limbs.

All trace-forms can be understood as built up by these four basic formal elements. The best way to convince oneself of this fact is to scribble on a piece of paper, in one uninterrupted line. Then, in examining the parts of the line, one notices that the scribble can be divided into sections which resemble the Arabic ciphers: 1 2 3. The form of these ciphers is related to the elements mentioned: 1 represents the *droit* or, if slightly curved, the *ouvert* while 2, with its double wave, corresponds to the *tortillé* and the 3 to the *rond*.

These forms in a scribble will sometimes be broken in an angular way so that the 2, for instance, appears as a zigzag: Z. They are often also badly proportioned in their parts, so that one of the curves of the 3, for instance, may be minute, and the rest of it extremely large. The movement which led to the scribbling can be observed as being composed exclusively of the three elements, namely the simple line, ╱ or ⌡, the double wave, ⌣⌢, and the round, ◯.

It is interesting to notice that all alphabets and signs for numbers and similar symbols are built up from these fundamental formal elements. For instance, as already mentioned, the first three Arabic ciphers, 1, 2 and 3, or characters occurring in Greek writing, such as the aspiration mark ‘, or the letters α, β, show the standard forms of bodily movement. Form is produced by the limbs of the body and is governed by their anatomical structure which permits only certain movements to be made arising from the functions of bending, stretching, twisting and combinations of these. This influences all writing and drawing activity of our hands and seems to restrict it to the use of the aforementioned four formal elements as a basis for shaping from which innumerable combinations can be made.

The four shapes are all parts or metamorphoses of one basic trace-form, the spiral. Parts of the standard scale in the preceding chapters are spiraloid curves. It is only through our "bodily perspective" that we see differences

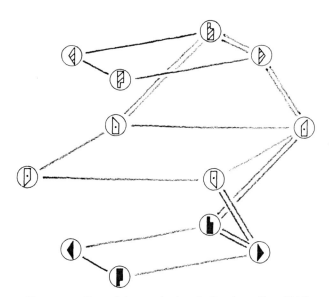

FIG. 31.—*Part of the standard-scale forming a "tortillé."*

in the spiraloid curvature of the line. We mentioned in the Introduction that man's impression of forms, when the motive power works within the body, is completely different from that received when he looks at them from an outside standpoint. We may call the view from within the "bodily perspective."

The trace-form illustrated in Fig. 31* which is half the standard scale described in Chapter VII gives, when performed, a clear feeling of a *tortillé* that is a winding, wave-like movement. In space, however, it is a spiral, or whorl, coiling around an axial line. In other words, seeing it from the outside, we distinguish clearly the spiraloid character, whilst from within it is felt as a wave-like form. This feeling is produced by the muscular interruption of the flow; in twisting the fore-arm the body is forced to change from a clockwise direction to a counter-clockwise direction, since our arms are not able to follow a spiral which circumscribes such a great part of the surface of the scaffolding without being twisted or turned.

Such detail in the feeling of form seems to have been studied by ancient peoples. The Greeks discovered rules for twisted lines, and traces of this ancient study can still be found in the tradition of classical ballet.

As we have seen, the body tends to follow a spiral or round pathway with a wave-like (*tortillé*) movement. A typically flat shape containing such waves is the figure 8. At a time much nearer to our own the mathematical law of this shape related to the geometry of curves was defined and the shape was called "lemniscate."†

There are various other combinations of movements which can be seen and understood in two different ways. For instance, if we repeat a circular movement with the right arm and step forward in a straight line, we produce a cylindrical spiral in space, rather than the simple circle it appears to us (*see* Fig. 32). Our awareness of the space-form actually being shaped can become more clear when we execute the movement and steps with eyes closed, concentrating on the formal flow of the line.

---

* Note that this trace-form and some of the illustrations of trace-forms which follow are related to the twelve "signal-points." These, when connected, form a cuboctahedron (*see* Chapter X, Fig. 41).

† The discovery of the lemniscate and its representation in algebraic form is attributed to Jacob Bernoulli, one of a famous family of Swiss mathematicians and a contemporary of Newton.

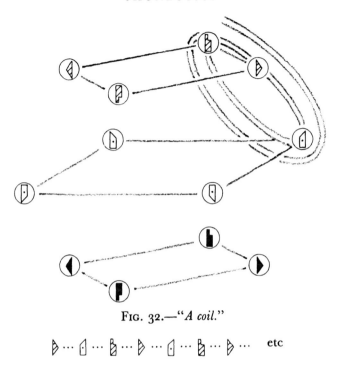

FIG. 32.—"*A coil.*"

♭ ⋯ ◁ ⋯ ♭ ⋯ ♭ ⋯ ◁ ⋯ ♭ ⋯ ♭ ⋯   etc

In Fig. 33 an interesting experiment is illustrated which takes a plastic spiral revolving around the centre ⊡ and projects it upon three co-ordinated planes.

The plastic spiral as seen from:

(*a*) ♭ projected upon a plane at ◁ forms a double *ouvert.*
(*b*) ♭   „   „ „ „ „ ♭   „   „ closed *rond.*
(*c*) ♭   „   „ „ „ „ ▮   „   „ *tortillé.*
(*d*) ◁ ⋯⋯⋯⋯⋯⋯⋯⋯⋯⋯⋯⋯   „   „ *rond.*

There are also differences of perception arising from dynamospheric influences. For instance, if we look towards the beginning of the trace-form our experience of its dynamism differs greatly from that gained when we look while we are moving, our experience of its dynamism differs greatly from that gained when we look towards the end of the same trace-form. If we watch experience. These three experiences might be called those of the past (looking towards the start of the movement), of the future (looking at the goal), and of the present (concentrating on the flow).

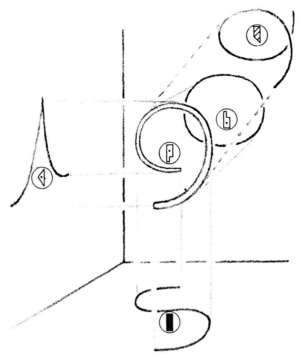

FIG. 33.—*A plastic spiral projected upon three co-ordinated planes.*

The experience of past, present or future, provoked by a bodily attitude (keeping our eyes focused on different spatial parts of a trace-form), offers us an aspect of time which differs basically from another aspect of time which we chiefly observe in a bodily action, namely quantities of speed: quickness and slowness. There is a fundamental difference between the placing of an action at a definite period within a span of time, that is to say at the beginning or end or at every instance of it, and the voluntarily shortening or lengthening of the extension between the beginning and end of an action by becoming quicker or slower in our movements. It seems that if we direct our attention towards the end of a trace-form or a path, we are more easily able to produce a quick movement, than when concentrating on the beginning of the trace-form, which seems to delay the flow. Recalling the investigations made in Chapter III, where we demonstrated the connection between the dimension extending between forward and backward and the degree of intensity of speed, we here have additional evidence of time as a spatial function.

Since the difference of impressions between looking from within, that is through bodily perspective, and looking from the outside seems to extend into dynamospheric experience, the sensations of time and dynamospheric realities underlying them demand a further and more explicit investigation. The few hints given here and in Chapter III do not pretend to exhaust the subject.

In becoming used to a new conception of time as a function of dynamic space which can be made visible by transferring it into kinespheric space, we must remember in what way the two conceptions of space differ for our bodily feeling. Kinespheric space is created by placing trace-forms around the body. In feeling dynamic space, the body is not aware primarily of fixed emplacements, but is driven by ever-changing dynamic impulses. They are associated with complicated spatial arrangements which result in indistinct, changeable feelings. Such feelings are the most usual in movements prompted by diagonal influences, which have a tendency to real mobility, bringing the body into situations which lack the perpendicular support. In diagonal inclinations our body flies or falls, while in dimensional tensions it is stable and always connected with the perpendicular support.

Our mental functions employ geometrical symbols to express orientation in space, but generally our feeling does not comprehend living movement within geometrical plasticity. Man can accustom himself to seeing and feeling the two differing views of body and mind simultaneously. This united perception demands training, so that mentally we can follow the new conception of time and understand more clearly the connections between the dynamosphere and kinesphere, while bodily we can make use of this knowledge when concerned with the training of expressive movement.

In every one-sided perception, especially when expressed in words only, there are serious pitfalls. This is also the case in the perception of a one-sided bodily perspective. In performing trace-forms which are combinations of the elements of the standard scale described in the last chapter, we are rarely fully conscious of their structure. Certain noddings of the head, or wavings of the hands, for instance, are often exact reproductions of the spatial order which rules the cluster or the standard scale surrounding it. We sometimes feel only the mood of sleepiness or excitement embodied in such a form (*see* Chapter VII) without becoming aware of the spatial structure which gives the mood its character, through the influence of height, depth and breadth and of the inclinations which appear in the shape of the movement. The placing in space, in different regions of the kinesphere, is felt only vaguely. For instance, we are inclined to notice the function of a limb in one of its characteristic zones, but not the details of its spatial orientation.

The same is the case with dynamospheric occurrences. They are comprehended by the mind as actions accompanied by feelings only, and not as inner spatial tensions with a determinative power. With the growing understanding of our kinaesthetic sense we may recognise that our nerves have the capacity for a genuine perception of spatial qualities.

It is surprising to realise that our conception of equilibrium is filled with a number of delusions. A most important way of attaining what we call equilibrium is found in the so-called movements of opposition. When one side of the body tends to go into one direction, the other side will almost automatically tend towards the contrary direction. We feel the loss of equilibrium and produce, often involuntarily, motions to re-establish balance. Such reactions lead for instance to a bodily attitude which is shown in Fig. 34.

The wish to establish equilibrium through symmetric movements is the

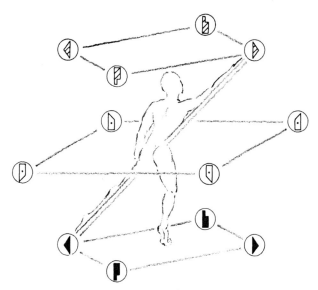

FIG. 34.—*Naturally equilibrated bodily attitude.*

left arm and leg: ◀ right arm: ▷

simplest manifestation of what we call harmony; the aim of this is not merely to hold the body in an upright position, but to achieve a unity of form, a wholeness, a completeness. Equilibrium through asymmetric movements has very many aspects. The influence of a flow of forms which disturbs a simple symmetry leads to asymmetric movements which must necessarily be completed by other asymmetric tensions or moves. The standard scale has two parts. The first series of six movements is situated in the opposite area of the kinesphere to that of the second series of six movements. The inclinations of the two series are parallel but they are followed in reversed directions. The standard scale, being the prototype of a chain which has equilibrium in its flow of forms, is the basis for the experience of spatial harmony.

In describing the standard scale, we noticed that the simple elements of orientation, the dimensions, seem to have in themselves certain equilibrating qualities. Movements containing dimensional tensions give, as mentioned above, a feeling of stability. This means that dimensions are primarily used in stabilising movement, in leading it to relative rest, to poses or pauses. Movements following space diagonals give, as also mentioned, a feeling of growing disequilibrium, or of losing balance. The balance is, so to speak, dissolved in the flow. Real mobility is, therefore, almost always produced by the diagonal qualities of an inclination. Since every movement is a composite of stabilising and mobilising tendencies, and since neither pure stability nor pure mobility exist, it will be the deflected or mixed inclinations which are the more apt to reflect trace-forms of living matter.

The mind always attempts to play the role of an outside observer, but because it exists within ourselves it is closely bound to the bodily perspective. The mind is in eternal conflict with those convincing facts which a genuine life-energy conveys to us. A certain rigidity of thinking arises which can be dispelled only by a more dynamic view of reality. Although in analysis we look at movement from the standpoint of an outside observer, we should try to feel it sympathetically from within. A mind trained to assist bodily perspective, instead of combating it, would give us a completely new outlook on movement and therefore on life.

It is true that our physical organism, the vehicle of the bodily perspective, appears and disappears in a pitiless rhythm. The human body is no more real than a flower, an object, a rock, or a star which appears, then vanishes after having existed for a day, a year, or hundreds of millions of years. Everything changes constantly without any true stability. Some elements may stay grouped together for a time, waxing and waning, but this individual gathering of the constituent elements is, in itself, in eternal motion.

We can therefore see that through the bodily perspective it is possible to reveal the connection between emotion within ourselves and movement outside ourselves. We can find more easily the different relationships between the paradoxical poles where our minds seem to become frozen. The bodily perspective with its uniting power will, however, not be prescribed as a universal remedy. It is necessary to emphasise, however, that to kill and neglect this essential faculty without understanding that it is a vitally necessary counterbalance to our mental delusions and their deteriorating effects is a dangerous tendency of our time. Therefore we need a new awareness and practice of this faculty.

Eighth fact of space-movement
Trace-forms have both an obvious and a hidden content. There are trace-forms within the body and outside it, and they are both closely interrelated, completing each other, as shadow and light. Hidden trace-forms are the "shadow-forms." They act in the dynamosphere as both the source and the producer of dynamic phenomena in the nerves, limbs and muscles of the body. All bending, turning and elevation of the body, the instrument of motion, is filled with dynamism, integrating the two elements, shadow and light. These primitive activities of dynamism lead to the most complex emotions we can feel and to the thoughts with which we try to grasp the essence of existence. The role of the bodily perspective is especially important in all investigations into movement and space.

CHAPTER IX

Stabilising and Mobilising of Trace-forms

IN investigating the secondary movements which in fact are muscular
tensions and which produce the dynamic variations of speed, force and
directional flux, we find two interesting sequences which are based on two
contrasting actions used in almost every activity, and which also appear in
the kinesphere.

When breaking a stick, or some other material, we are sometimes obliged
to overcome its resistance by a turning or twisting movement. With the help
of this movement we are able finally to separate it into two parts. We can
also use a twisting movement to join together ropes or wires, for instance,
but they will not hold together permanently unless we also carry out the
movement of tying the two parts into a knot.

The tying or twisting of a cord into a knot demands a concentration both
in muscle and mind; it is an action which can be performed only by human
beings, and not by animals. The untying or untwisting, which is to separate, and the contrary, the tying or twisting into a knot, which means to unite,
both lead to completely different inner and outer attitudes. The tying is
directed towards one central point, while the untying creates polarity.

In moving outwards towards the boundaries of the kinesphere, we usually
employ such untying or untwisting movements. Our natural structure provides the capacity to twist by making it possible, when turning the fore-arm,
to cross the two bones, the radius and ulna. One aim in reaching outward
is to create a distance between the centre of our body and the ends of our
limbs. The movement will be an opening or unfolding one and will bring
about a tension between two directions, the centre and a point on the
boundary. (*See also* scattering and gathering movements in Chapter V.)

In moving inwards towards the centre of our body we follow trace-forms
which resemble knots. Characteristic of these are the crossing and inter-

92

weaving of our arms over the chest and the movement is one of closing or wrapping.

A circle of string can be twisted into the form of a figure eight (8), and this figure eight can be untwisted into the original circle. A knot in the circle of string cannot be untwisted as long as the circle remains uncut.

Our movement sometimes traces circles which can easily be transformed into the shape of a figure eight and other twisted shapes. At other times they are knotted, so to speak, and can be transmuted into other lines only after being cut by a complete stop and by a new impulse. Here we have examples of discontinued or interrupted movements.

There are psychological implications in these facts and here perhaps we are on the borderline of penetrating the emotional content of movement. It is quite possible to describe in words the interrelations between the movements of the body and the functions of the mind in single significant movements, but in dance, the trace-forms and their dynamic unfolding must speak for themselves. The spectator will at first be surprised, perhaps, at the harmony existing between the various parts of the shapes of trace-forms and the dynamic sequences which express the state of mind and the meaning of the whole movement.

By concentrating on the structure of the bare trace-form, on the one hand, and by practising the dynamic stresses which the trace-form demands, on the other, we are able in time to analyse the formal structure of a movement, as well as the nuances of the flow which underlie the meaning of the structure. There are some basic qualities of shape-form which can be explained in words. We see, for instance, that phrasing of the flow of movement reigns supreme in dance. A single movement is not dance, no matter how dance-like it might be in its form and rhythm, or however beautiful or expressive it might seem. The lasting, uninterrupted flow of organised movement phrases is true dance. Some single movements can be "dance-movements" perhaps, in contrast to "every-day movements" or those of play, sport and so on, but they are not yet a complete dance.

Dance is the transition into a world in which the illusory, static appearances of life are transformed into clear spatial dynamism. Awareness of this spatial world and its exploration open up a horizon of unexpected breadth. From the simplest motion to the artistic creation of dancing, the flowing stream of movement expresses dynamic space, the basis of all existence. All movement emerges from this infinite abyss and disappears into it again.

Dynamic space, with its terrific dance of tensions and discharges is the fertile ground in which movement flourishes. Movement is the life of space. Dead space does not exist, for there is neither space without movement nor movement without space. All movement is an eternal change between binding and loosening, between the creation of knots with the concentrating and uniting power of binding, and the creation of twisted lines in the process of untying and untwisting. Stability and mobility alternate endlessly.

Stability in dance does not mean either complete rest or absolute stillness. Stability has the tendency to facilitate temporary and relative quietude which is equilibrium. Mobility on the contrary means a tendency towards vivid, flowing movement, leading to a temporary loss of equilibrium. For instance, in a flying turning leap (*grand jeté en tournant*) the whole body is in a mobile state. When the jump is terminated and the feet touch the floor again, there is a tendency towards quietude and equilibrium. Stability follows the former state of mobility.

Stability is not always guaranteed, however, by the act of standing on the feet. An exaggerated, wide circle, performed with the upper part of the body can provoke a temporary imbalance, or mobility, which is afterwards retransformed into stability. All our steps and gestures of the arms are rhythmical changes between stability and mobility.

Movements with axial counter-tensions are generally stable. Surface movements which affect the whole body promote mobility if they are not counteracted by polar tendencies. However, surface movements are generally executed by gestures of the limbs only when the axis of a trace-form does not play a prominent role in the tension of the body. The axial counter-tension is almost always hidden in an inner shadow-form, which provokes the characteristic tensing of the muscles, which we call strength, or, in a wider sense, dynamism. The shadow-forms are composed of the elements of the dynamosphere, as we have already seen. Their relationships are so infinitely manifold that they cannot be enumerated, but each of them can be understood as a characteristic stage of a harmonic development.

There is a veritable chain of inclinations which could be called a standard scale of the dynamosphere and which has two different forms. One of these is a knot and the other is a twisted circle.

A standard scale of the dynamosphere evolves around a diagonal but it is clearly orientated towards one of the two directions of the diagonal. An image which can facilitate our understanding is that a standard scale of the dynamosphere does not form either a cluster or a girdle, like a standard scale of the kinesphere, but a kind of basket, the bottom of which is orientated towards one direction of a diagonal, while its opening is orientated towards the other direction of the same diagonal. The three transversals of the basket occupy half the scaffolding, so to speak, and do not transgress to the other side which is divided off by the girdle around the diagonal. The other parts are symmetric forms all of the same structure, but they are differently orientated. Yet this basket is not regular or symmetric, but has a spiral form like that of a snail shell. This can be seen in Fig. 35..

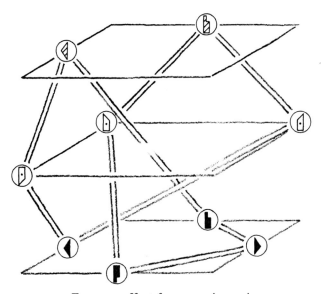

FIG. 35.—*Knot-form around an axis.*

Axis: ▌ ··· ▨
Chain of the knot:

The knot-form of a dynamospheric standard scale shown in Fig. 35 is a knotted circle and contains nine links. Three of them are transversals and six are surface-lines. It is, therefore, a mixed scale and differs in this respect from the standard scales of the kinesphere.

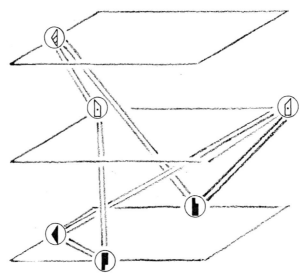

FIG. 36.—*Chain of a simple twisted circle.*

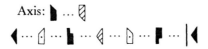

The simple twist-form of a standard scale in the dynamosphere illustrated in Fig. 36 is also a mixed scale and contains the same transversals. The six surface-lines of the knot are replaced by three others. Its tension is, so to speak, simplified and contains only six links. It also has a spiral tendency.

The transversals in the knot:

are perpendicular to each other, which means that they have a tendency towards stability. The other lines are surface-lines three of which are parts of the corresponding girdle:

The remaining three links are:

and each of these is perpendicular to a girdle link, thus reinforcing stability.

The chain of the knot can be followed in a clockwise as well as in a counter-clockwise direction. The clockwise path has a narrowing tendency, the counter-clockwise path a widening tendency. The chain cannot be un-twisted as long as the circle is not cut by an interruption of movement.

Replacing the six surface-lines by three others, which lead to three points of the corresponding cluster, we get the simple twisted form of the standard scale of the dynamosphere which is shown in Fig. 36.

The chain can be untwisted without being cut, and so has the possibility of evolving continuously in ever-new shapes. The restriction of evolution in the knot causes its stability. The freedom to evolve gives the twist its mobility.

Certain ornamental torsions which we like to execute with our hands at the ends of radiating movements, show clearly the intercepting function of a knot-line, which leads to a pause (*tour de main*). The beginning of a move-ment, on the contrary, is often characterised by a twisted contraction from which it flows outward in an untwisting, opening manner.

We may conclude that movement can spring from a more or less percep-tible inner twist and can end in a more or less perceptible inner knot. The "inner" refers in this case to the kinaesthetic awareness within the moving limb, and not to the centre of the kinesphere. The final knot must be dis-solved into a simple twist, before the new impulse can become visible.

An intermediary stage between the knot and the simple twisted line is the lemniscate.* Knot-lines and twist-lines can form the edge of lemniscatic bands. Such bands have not clearly distinguishable inside or outside

* Laban adopted the term "lemniscate" and extended its connotation to a twisted band-like trace-form in three-dimensional space. Such trace-forms he found naturally evolving in movement through the structure of the human body, particularly of the upper limbs, whose use is predominant in both operational and expressive functions. The word lemniscate is derived from the Latin *lemniscus* (band), and Laban used it exclusively in the above-mentioned sense.

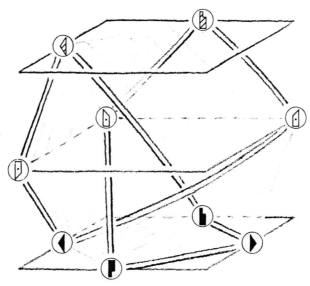

FIG. 37.—*Lemniscatic band of the knot.*

surfaces. They are twisted band-circles. When we observe people move, it
frequently seems as if they have the desire to nestle in a curved plane or an
arched band, or to stroke it. Planes, bands and also lemniscates can be
recognised by their double-line trace-forms concurrently made by two parts
of the moving limb or the trunk. This is like a "duet" of two parts of the
body just as in two-part singing. The knotted form of the dynamospheric
standard scale can be felt as a lemniscatic band. This band, as stated, has
no division between inside and outside; it has a one-sided surface with one
continuous line forming its edge. We have to move along the whole band
twice in order to return to the point of departure, twisting at the same time.*

* The mathematician and astronomer A. F. Moebius (1790–1868) discovered a surface
which he described as having no "other side," i.e. a surface from the one side of which one
can get to its other without crossing an edge. It is called the "Moebius Band" or "Moebius
Strip." Laban's lemniscate corresponds exactly to this description, but he heard of it only
early in the 1950s after he had already worked and experimented with this strange kind
of circuit for many years in relation to the qualitative aspect of human movement. It is,
however, conceivable that as a boy he came across certain magic tricks based on mathematical curiosities, as these were fashionable party-games in his youth.

Fig. 37 is a knotted dynamospheric standard scale showing lemniscatic character. The signal-points of the double-line trace-form which are touched simultaneously are written one under the other.

The possibilities of lemniscatic rings or bands are innumerable. They are of a dynamospheric rather than of a kinespheric character. Knotted circles as well as twisted circles can be lemniscates but are not always necessarily so.

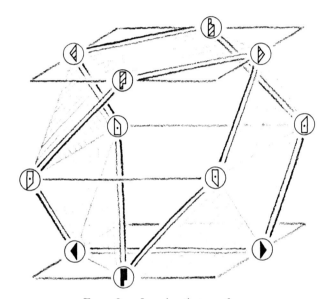

FIG. 38.—*Lemniscatic trace-form.*

Fig. 38 is an example of a twisted lemniscate which has no knot. The asymmetric twist of this line with one transversal ❙ ... ▯ and ten surface-lines is a very large, peripheral form.

Some other lemniscates are directly bound to the centre and they are the shadow-kernels of seven-ring sequences. (*See* seven-ring sequences and bodily zones, in Chapter II. Also similarity to acoustics in Chapter XI.) The shadow-kernel-lemniscate of seven-rings consists of two half diameters, one transversal and three surface-lines. They are at the same time the kernels of the primitive tetrahedroid tensions of simple bodily poses (*see* Chapter II).

Kernels are often projected into the kinesphere, and become outer movements, such as lead to tetrahedroid poses, for instance. They are transformed into inner energies and then appear as dynamic qualities. Outer
trace-forms can become kernels or shadow-forms and awaken an amazing
number of nuances of dynamic potential. Afterwards they can again be
liberated and so enrich the kinespheric life.

Different stages of an inner happening, such as binding and loosening,
often have a dramatic expression. "Dramatic" is used here in the sense of
a struggle between contrasting forces which appear in the flux of movement. The struggling tendencies build and destroy forms with varied
rhythms. This dramatic action is the real content of artistic movements in
acting and dancing. The various shape-forms become the letters, syllables
and words of the language of movement.

It is a secondary consideration from the point of view of choreutics
whether or not this fight and harmony of trace-forms have certain comprehensible content, such as feelings, thoughts and actions, in themselves. A
definite movement with a definite trace-form is always connected with
inner happenings such as feelings, reflections, determinations of the will and
other emotional impulses.

Ninth fact of space-movement

Movement is man's magic mirror, reflecting and creating the inner life
in and by visible trace-forms, and also reflecting and creating the visible
trace-forms in and by the inner life. The simplest visible element of this
paradoxical and startling operation is the play between axial-stable and
surface-mobile bodily movements, or in other words, the struggle between
the binding power of a knot and the loosening power of an untwisting line
with an intermediary lemniscate.

Extreme narrowness of movement approaches central dynamic functions,
and there is a change into infinitely small shapeless forms. Width loses
itself in the infinitely large band of an outer lemniscatic plane which no
longer has either visible or tangible space character. The interplay between
these two infinities is the last stage of comprehension of the paradoxical
mixture of motion and emotion which man can attain with his brain.
Bodily experience goes further. Life felt as enjoyment of activity glitters in
myriads of trace-forms which can become conscious and vitally effective.

CHAPTER X

Cubic and Spheric Forms of the Scaffolding

THE principles of choreutics can easily be developed by taking the cube as the basis of our spatial orientation. The conception of the cube as a basis is not a compromise but a fundamental principle of our orientation in space. In practice, harmonious movement of living beings is of a fluid and curving nature which can be more clearly symbolised by a scaffolding closer to a spheric shape. However, for general observation and notation of trace-forms, this variation is not vitally important.

Signs for the signal-points of the scaffolding adapted to human movement are the same as in the usual cubic orientation. Only refined observation, and above all, practice in bodily movement can give knowledge of a variation of the basic orientation in space. It is the construction of the body which demands a modification of the purely cubic aspect of the directional scheme of the kinesphere, and alters slightly the emplacement of the twelve signal-points when the body moves.

Thus placing the arms: ◁ ▷

and the feet: ◀ ▶

we notice that the quadrangle which is marked by these four points is not a square, as in the cube, but a rectangle, higher than it is broad. This means that the diameters leading to ◁ and ▷ at one end, and to ▶ and ◀ at the other, are a little nearer to each other, and thus nearer also to the dimension ▯ ... ▮ situated between them.

The same is the case with: ▯ and ▮

which are nearer to: ▯

as well as: ▯ and ▮

which are nearer to: ▯

Similarly: ⟨ and ⟩

                    are nearer to: ⟩

                        while: ⟨ and ⟩

                    are nearer to: ⟨

We therefore do not name the twelve directional points of the scaffolding according to the level towards which the movement radiates (as introduced in Chapter I) but according to the main extension of the rectangular planes. Thus, in the plane extending mainly from ▯ to ▮ we distinguish:

high right, ⟩.; *high* left, ⟨
deep right, ▶ ; *deep* left, ◀

in the plane extending mainly from ▯ to ▯ we distinguish:

forward high, ▯ ; *forward* deep, ▮
backward high, ▯ ; *backward* deep, ▮

in the plane extending mainly from ⟩ to ⟨ we distinguish:

right forward, ⟨ ; *right* backward, ⟨
left forward, ⟩ ; *left* backward, ⟩

The emplacement and names of the dimensionals and diagonals are not altered. (Further explanations are given in Part II.)

The resulting plastic form which is built up by the modified diameters is an icosahedron. This is a polyhedron which is not among inorganic crystals. The first person to describe it was the Greek philosopher, Plato. Only recently science has discovered the appearance of the icosahedron in certain structural relationships within the organic world.* It is very

---

* Recent research has made more discoveries in this direction, especially in connection with the structure of certain viruses.

interesting that the movements of man should evolve within the same form in a completely natural way.

One can conceive of a kind of dynamic crystallography* of human movement in which spatial tensions and transformations are scientifically examined in a way similar to that undertaken when investigating those which occur in the building up of matter. Amongst the fundamental principles that must be taken into account in this science, the most pertinent to our present considerations are the two following:

    1. That the dimensional directions form the corners of an octahedron (Fig. 39).

    2. That the diagonal directions form the corners of a cube (Fig. 40).

There are various chemical compounds which crystallise in these two forms and their atoms are arranged in a similar manner.

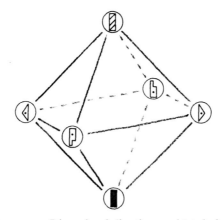

FIG. 39.—*Dimensional directions and octahedron.*

These two regularly structured crystals are dynamic variations of the simplest plastic form, the tetrahedron, from which all other polyhedric or crystalline forms derive. The transformation into a new form can be imagined in dynamic crystallography to be effected by movements of the edges of both their inner and outer planes. Such deviations are caused by pressing and rotating movements so that one is transformed into another.

* Crystallography is the science which deals with the system of forms amongst crystals.

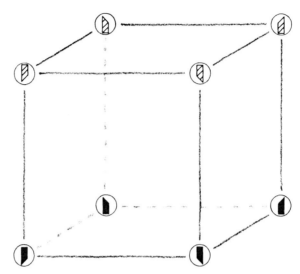

FIG. 40.—*Diagonal directions and cube.*

The intermediary form between the octahedron and the cube is the cuboctahedron. Its deflected inclinations bring about the cuboctahedral scaffolding (Fig. 41).

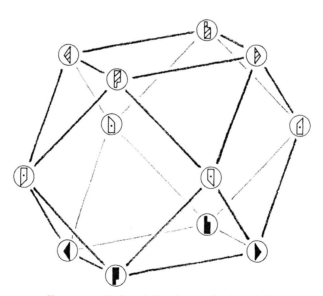

FIG. 41.—*Deflected directions and cuboctahedron.*

The points of an icosahedral scaffolding are the same as those of the cuboctahedron, with the deviations already mentioned:

◁ and ▷ are nearer to ⊘ = hl and hr

◀ ,, ▶ ,, ,, ,, ▮ = dl ,, dr

⬧ ,, ❙ ,, ,, ,, ⬦ = fh ,, fd

⬨ ,, ❙ ,, ,, ,, ⬧ = bh ,, bd

◁ ,, ⬧ ,, ,, ,, ▷ = rf ,, rb

⬧ ,, ⬦ ,, ,, ,, ◁ = lf ,, lb

Fig. 42 shows the adaptation of the cuboctahedron to a more spheric form, the icosahedron.

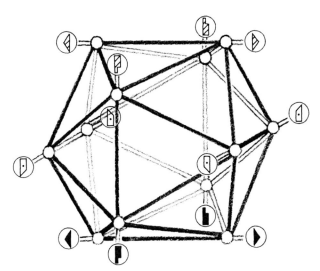

FIG. 42.—*The icosahedron as related to cuboctahedral corner points.*

We can understand all bodily movement as being a continuous creation of fragments of polyhedral forms. The body itself, in its anatomical or crystalline structure, is built up according to the laws of dynamic crystallisation. Old magic rites have preserved a great deal of knowledge about these laws. Plato's description of the regular solids in the *Timaeus* is based on such ancient knowledge. He followed the traditions of Pythagoras who was the first, as far as is known, to have investigated harmony in European civilisation.

In order to study harmony of movement we must consider the relations between the architecture of the human body and the spatial structure
of the kinesphere. Anatomically it has been shown that the body and its
limbs can be moved only in certain restricted areas of the kinesphere, which
we called "zones" of the limbs. In these the moving limbs describe certain
angles of rotations and flexion. The size of the angle is determined by the
individual structure of the joints. Anatomists have investigated the exact
size of the angles which each limb can make, and in the movement habits of
humans the following angles can readily be observed.

Normally from a balanced carriage the head bends forward and backward at an angle of approximately 45°. The movement requires more
agility to produce further bending.

Generally we turn the head to either side at an angle of approximately
30°; turning further, as when looking over one's shoulder, requires the participation of an increased area of the body.

It is remarkable that the complete bending angle of the head is approximately a right angle, the angle through which we pass from one dimension
of space to another, and that the complete turning angle of the head is
about 60°, the angle of an equilateral triangle. The surface of an icosahedron consists of equilateral triangles.

In everyday life the flexion and extension of the vertebral column achieves
an angle of approximately 72° (6 × 12). The angle of 72° is an angle between transversals and a surface-line in the icosahedron. The turning of the
hips also comes near to 72°.

All these figures are averages, arrived at by measurements taken from
a large number of people in "normal" living conditions, and these correlate
with measurements taken from lifeless human bodies. Deviations from these
averages were found, in corpses, to be apparently not more than 2%. Living
beings are often inhibited in reaching the average span in their movements,
either through clumsiness or psychological reasons. Nevertheless, the deviation from the average was seldom more than 5%. An excessive capacity to
bend or turn was rarely found in normal cases, and then the deviation was
not more than an average of 2%.

When we wish to touch a point on the floor behind ourselves, for instance
▌ , we must employ a number of interrelated movements. The most important of these are, in this case, flexing the knees, turning the pelvis with

rotation and extension of dorsal and lumbar vertebrae, whilst reaching back and down with the arm. This movement therefore is very complicated, but between the angles of the component moves there is a precise relationship which is determined by a law—the law of harmony in movement. If we disobey this law, we shall then succeed in reaching the desired point only by means of incredible distortions and with the greatest difficulty. Obedience to this law engenders harmony of movement.

Every point of the kinesphere can be reached with any one limb, which means that together they have a reaching span of 360° when helped by certain determinable contributory movements from other parts of the body. These contributory movements also have a limited range which is determined by the degrees of their angles. Comparing the angles in the icosahedron with the angles occurring in the movements of the body in normal everyday use, we can come to the following conclusions and form the following scheme:

In the Body:		*In the Icosahedron:*
Flexion and extension angle of the head: (atlanto-occipital joint)	45°	Angle between dimensionals and diameters.
Rotating angle for the head: (at atlanto=axial joint)	60°	Angle between the neighbouring surface-lines and also triangles formed by transversals.
Turning angle of the vertebral column:	60°	
Tilting angle of the pelvic girdle:	60°	
Angle between flexion and extension of the vertebral column:	72°	Angle at the base of a triangle formed by transversals and a surface-line.
Turning angle of the hips:	72°	
Abduction of shoulder joint or lifting angle of the arm sideways (without movement of the scapula).	90°	Angle between two dimensions.
Flexion and extension of shoulder joint or lifting angle of the stretched arm forward and backward (without rotating the scapula).	108°	Angle between two non-neighbouring surface-lines (belonging to a five-ring).

The correspondence between the angles of the icosahedron and the maximum angles through which the limbs move is quite astonishing. They appear to be either the same, or exactly half, or double, of those mentioned. It is also interesting that the proportion between the length of the dimensional and diagonal transversals of the icosahedron and the length of its surface-lines follows the law of the Golden Section. This ratio is found in the measurement of the angles and constituent lines occurring in the rectangles of the three-dimensional planes and in the pentagonal structure of the five-rings (see Part II). The Golden Section is also considered to be the ruling proportion between all the different parts of the perfectly built human body and throughout the ages its mathematical law has been closely connected with aesthetics.* This shows an infinite series of re-divisions in which each small part has the same relation to the larger part as the larger part has to the whole. It was first discovered by the Ancient Egyptians and used by them in their buildings and other works of art. Later the Greeks worked out the mathematics of its proportion and Pythagoras proved that the human body is built according to the Golden Section.

The Greeks made widespread use of this discovery in their sculptures as is evident in the works of Phidias and his contemporary Polycletus, two of the foremost Athenian sculptors of the fifth century B.C. whose statues represent the ideal human and divine form. They also applied the underlying theories to the construction of their temples. Medieval builders of churches and cathedrals worked much in the same way, and from the time of the Renaissance Leonardo da Vinci's analysis of the human figure based on the Golden Proportion has been well known.

In an icosahedron every inclination with a stable tendency has in its immediate neighbourhood an inclination with a labile tendency so that the harmonic step from one to the other is much easier than in a cubic form. This is the important characteristic of a scaffolding which approaches a spheric shape and in addition the icosahedron has a great wealth of lemniscatic traceforms (see Chapter IX).

* It should be emphasised that the idea of using the icosahedron as the scaffolding of the kinesphere in practising movement did not originate because of the knowledge of the relationships mentioned above, but arose spontaneously from the study of movement and dance. The present systematic description therefore is not imposed from without, but is based on the inherent laws of natural movement, which gradually came to light in the author's professional activity as a dancer and dance-teacher.

CUBIC AND SPHERIC FORMS OF THE SCAFFOLDING   109

The dynamics of movement give rise to shapes which can often be felt as intermediary stages between the different crystalline forms. They can be organised in the cuboctahedric scaffolding which derives from the three simple polyhedral forms of the tetrahedron, the octahedron, and the cube as well as in the icosahedron which, as mentioned above, is a dynamic variation of the cuboctahedron.

Dynamic crystallography provides a useful basis for the understanding of the changes from one scaffolding to another, as well as of the transition from a smaller scaffolding to a larger one and vice versa, which constitutes extension and contraction between "X" and "И."

The different shapes into which matter crystallises can be described and understood through the means of choreutic symbols. Structural arrangements of minerals and organic matter show forms in which the inclinations, natural sequences and standard scales are clearly traced. Since these relationships appear to exist everywhere in nature, there will be little room for exceptions.

It will be interesting to determine differences or deviations occurring in the standard forms of inorganic and organic matter. We can easily see one of these when we compare, for instance, the girdle of the cuboctahedron with the girdle of an icosahedron.

The girdle of a cuboctahedron is flat and lies in a plane. The girdle of an icosahedron is slightly bent and the connections of the diametrically opposite signal-points produce a wave-like shape around the centre in which they intersect. The energy needed for such an unfolding into a third dimension, through bulging and retracting, is characteristic of the organic world. In highly organised living beings this energy is supplemented by an accentuated dynamism which is released foremost through mental-emotional channels. The various compounds of mental and emotional energy which the individual living being is able to form and to link can be observed in his movements and described in dynamospheric terms. The girdle of the dynamosphere may be compared with, but not exemplified by, a cuboctahedral or icosahedral girdle. Perhaps a girdle in lemniscatic form might be more appropriate to the dynamosphere. This may be clarified through an analysis of the seven-rings which are super-zones of the arms (*see* Chapter II) and also of the shadow-kernels of these super-zones.

Tenth fact of space-movement

A crystal seems to be limited in its shape by the interplay of three elements: corners, edges and polygons. A dynamospheric form is limited in its shape by the interplay of four elements, namely: corners, edges, polygons and polyhedra.

The girdle of a dynamospheric scaffolding cannot be expressed—as is the girdle of the cuboctahedral scaffolding—by a polygon, that is, by a plane bordered by a line. Nor can it be expressed by a polyhedral structure, bordered by planes, as is the girdle of the icosahedron. A new kind of tension appears. We can capture it in the image of a space-form which extends between polyhedra.

There is a series of bodily exercises which bring a very real sensation of these hitherto nameless space-forms. The teaching of dance in all periods abounds in such exercises as the space-forms are mainly of an expressive nature. Human movement has only occasionally been investigated from this point of view, but can be shown to consist of tensions within space-forms. This demonstration has its roots in the discovery of harmonic relations between vibrations, already known in acoustics, as well as in spectral-analysis and now also in choreutics.

The part of this study which is easy to approach will be touched upon in the next chapter in so far as it relates to our main theme.

(NOTE: the conception of a new possibility of spatial arrangements and relationships which appears in organic life and movement is of immense importance. The description of such forms was approached in Chapter IX, when we spoke about knots, twists and lemniscates. To mention further details would exceed the bounds of what is only an introductory account.)

CHAPTER XI

Choreutic Shapes Performed by the Body

ALTHOUGH in a dance composition it may be useful to give specific suggestions regarding the use of the limbs in executing a certain trace-form, it is not necessary to do this for a simple performance of choreutic chains. Each choreutic chain can be followed in various ways by the body and its limbs. The same applies to dynamic nuances which appear when performing a chain. In dance composition, the rhythm and the use of the various nuances of force and directional flux has to be given in a much more explicit manner than that given in suggestions for performing choreutic chains. In these it is useful from many points of view to omit entirely all precise instructions as to bodily execution and dynamic intentions, for it will be both advantageous and instructive for the performer to experiment and find for himself the most harmonious way of executing simple forms.

There are general harmonies resulting from the structure of the human body, and individual harmonies which come from both the physiological and psychological state of the individual. Some restrictions in the free use of the zones can be caused by lack of exercise, and this lack can be caused by bodily laziness, weakness or by psychological hindrances, such as anxiety and timidity. A healthy human being can have complete control of his kinesphere and dynamosphere, but there are considerations such as individual expressiveness or taste which can influence the personal conception of harmony in movement. Graceful movements will suit one person more than vital or bizarre movements, or the contrary may be the case. This is a question of individual temperament; some will prefer narrow and restrained movements, others may like to move freely in space, and so forth.

The essential thing is that we should neither have preference for nor avoid certain movements because of physical or psychical restrictions. We should be able to do every imaginable movement and then select those which seem to be the most suitable and desirable for our own nature. These can be found only by each individual himself. For this reason, practice of the free use of kinetic and dynamic possibilities is of the greatest advantage. We should be acquainted both with the general movement capacities of a healthy body and mind and with the specific restrictions and capacities resulting from the individual structure of our own bodies and minds.

In general, it will be advantageous to try to feel trace-forms in the trunk first and to awaken the kinetic force in the limbs afterwards. This procedure guarantees the connection between kinetism and dynamism, and it furthers the integration of body and mind in movement.

Designing trace-forms in the air with the extremities only can lead to a kind of external form-writing. Understanding forms with the brain only, or responding to them with feeling only, without perceptible bodily movement, has the disadvantage of giving a purely intellectual or sentimental pleasure, without the benefit of their integrating power. The integrating power of movement is perhaps its most important value for the individual. There are, however, certain fundamental laws which can guide the performer and teacher. They derive from the facts described in the ten previous chapters.

We must take into consideration:

I. The general principles of *orientation in space*.

II. The *zones of the limbs* which give a hint as to which limb can be used in certain trace-forms, or its sections. At first it is wise to avoid the super-zones, or to employ them consciously as a combination of different limb-zones.

III. The *dynamic value* of shadow-forms. When executing one and the same trace-form with different dynamic expression the performer will notice that various accompanying shadow-forms appear. One of them will be felt to be the most suitable for that particular trace-form.

IV. The *natural sequences in the kinesphere*, deriving from everyday activities such as fighting, running, swimming, or from movements which resemble such activities. A trace-form can thus have a kind of mimetic or action content. It will be helpful to discover the defensive or aggressive content in a trace-form, although this primitive contrast does not embrace the infinite variations of actions. Thoughtfulness and emotion will be awakened through the careful performance of a trace-form. The mimetic content, however, should never be expressed through conventional gestures, such as pointing to an object with a finger, or copying any activity of everyday life, but should be transformed into an expressive or symbolic movement. In this way, the essence of an action movement may be found. The physiological and psychological value of this discovery of the essence of movement can be enormous. It may be found to relate even to ethical awareness, with all its profound significance in life.

V. The *functions of the body and its limbs*. These are very numerous, especially in movements through combined zones. We cannot reach certain points of the larger kinesphere without bending, twisting, kneeling, lying, jumping, and so forth. The smaller kinesphere felt in the trunk does not demand such composite movements. In transposing a trace-form from its most minute extension in the trunk to its greatest extension outside it, we find an extraordinarily rich range of possibilities in the use of the limbs and indeed of the whole body.

VI. The *natural chain of inclinations in the dynamosphere* can bring an awareness of *the changes of mood* and their transitions, and of the most suitable sequences in shadow-trace-forms. In filling trace-forms with dynamic life, one will notice that they do not only contain one typical dynamic quality, but that some demand certain sequences of dynamic nuances. A trace-form can be charged with dynamic nuances and can also be lacking in this respect. Simplicity here, as in all movement, is the guiding law.

VII. *The standard scales in the kinesphere* give a basic scheme for the different *qualities of inclinations*. This means that a trace-form, or its component parts, can be understood as parts of a girdle around the scaffolding, or of a cluster which traverses the scaffolding axially. Other sequences of movement are related to these basic forms. Standard scales of movement demand certain dynamic and bodily forms of expression. It is advantageous to learn to respond to these demands by intuitive feeling and afterwards by a conscious control.

VIII. Awareness of *bodily perspective* will assist in the discrimination between spatial feeling and understanding and the spontaneous activity of our limbs. Following trace-forms in their pure kinespheric form can be the first step towards meaningful use of the limbs. Later the faculty of discrimination between the quality of the inner impulse and the outer form which is present in all movements will grow. The definite and joyful execution of an integrated movement will be the final result.

IX. Awareness of the *standard scales in the dynamosphere* leads to the very source of movement. The *binding-loosening processes* in nature, leading to change between stability and mobility, are not only reflected in the essential forms which our movements take, but they are also the basic content of the language of movement. In order to read and speak this language one must experience its alphabet which is hidden in both the kinespheric and dynamospheric standard scales. The part of this language of movement which can be said in words has already been attempted in previous chapters, but it must be understood that spatial, bodily and psychological analysis cannot replace the integration which takes place during movement. The hint given above, that the discovery of the essence of movement might relate to ethical awareness, is not less important than the hints given about the healthy use of the body and its limbs.

X. The *movements* of our body follow rules corresponding to those of mineral *crystallisations* and structures of organic compounds. The shape which possibly offers the most natural and harmonious tracks for our movements is the *icosahedron*. It contains a rich series of combined inner and outer trace-lines with dimensional connections provoking "stable," i.e. easily equilibrated, movements as well as diagonal connections provoking disequilibrating movements. Trace-forms of movements are, however, never complete crystal-patterns, but awareness of a harmonious flow resulting from crystalline tendencies increases pleasure in skill. The main practical purpose of our mobility is the lifting, shifting and transporting of objects to various places in our surroundings, or the transforming of their shape or constitution into new forms or shapes. The final aim, however, is to sustain or promote the processes concerned with the structural arrangements which happen within our body-mind. Any action or any form of behaviour unfolds within the bounds of dynamic crystallisation.

The integration of body and mind through movement occurs in the free performance of choreutic shapes. There is no limit to the possibilities of the study and practice of choreutics. It penetrates every human action and reaction, since all actions and reactions spring from movement within us. In the domain of the arts this fact becomes especially clear.

There are the visible arts such as architecture, sculpture and painting in which the trace-forms are fixed through the movement of drawing and the shaping of different materials. There are the audible arts, such as music and oratory (including the speaking of poetry), in which the trace-forms of bodily movements give shape to the sounds and rhythms, which characterise ideas and emotions.

It is probable that dance and architecture are the two basic arts of man from which the others derive. We can build three-dimensional or plastic models of trace-forms in which the whole line of a movement is seen. While in actual movements, point after point of the trace-forms vanish into the past, future movements appear in the inventive imagination simultaneously, as plastic entities. It is evident that some of the "snail-shells of the soul," as someone jokingly called the models of dance trace-forms, have a construction very similar to modern plastic art and architecture. The first inner vision of a choreutic shape and the first inner vision of an architectural creation or an abstract drawing have a great resemblance. The invention of an architectural, plastic or pictorial form is, in reality, a choreutic phrase.

This phrase is constructed out of changing spatial tendencies. It can be seen how the directions change when one draws a well known symbol such as a letter of the alphabet or a number. The same symbol can be drawn not only on paper, but shaped plastically in three-dimensional space. Symbols, both known and unknown, constitute the spatial melodies of dance.

Movements of the dances of primitive tribes and certain refined movements of later epochs sometimes, perhaps unconsciously, followed stylised contours of geometrical symbols, real objects, or living beings. To understand and remember a trace-form, it may often be useful to know what we shape (e.g. a triangle), or to know what familiar contour the trace-form of our movements resembles (e.g. a cave or a worm). The variety of closed circuits such as chains of surface-lines is enormous and includes almost all possible forms which the imagination can construct. It also has an important meaning if a chain traces particular paths along a spatial form.

We can follow the surface-lines of an octahedral, cuboctahedral or icosahedral scaffolding of the kinesphere in an uninterrupted chain, and it is possible to spread each plastic circuit into a plane and open it out into a circle. The circle, in fact, is a polygon consisting of different links as does

the scaffolding of the kinesphere which has an angular character because
of its surface-lines.

Fig. 43 shows the process of unfolding an uninterrupted circuit of an
octahedron at first spreading it into a plane and finally forming a polygon of
twelve sides (dodecagon).

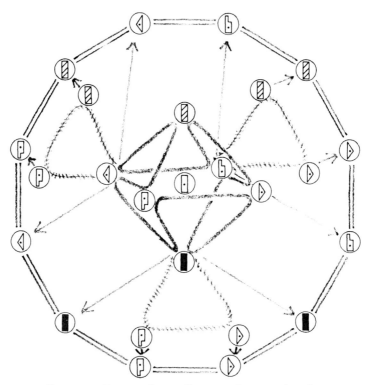

FIG. 43.—*Process of spreading an uninterrupted surface-
line of an octahedron on a plane.*

Figs. 44a and 44b shows an uninterrupted surface-line of an icosahedral
scaffolding spread into a plane. It can be further unfolded to form a polygon
of 36 sides.

Borders of polygons have rhythmic and harmonic relations which
are aspects of the harmonic life of choreutic trace-forms. When the
plastic form of an octahedron is unfolded harmonically, as the example
given in Fig. 43 shows, fundamental scales are displayed in both the sequence
of the links around the border and in the sequence of the twelve-cornered
star which can be inscribed within it. An analogy with harmonic relations

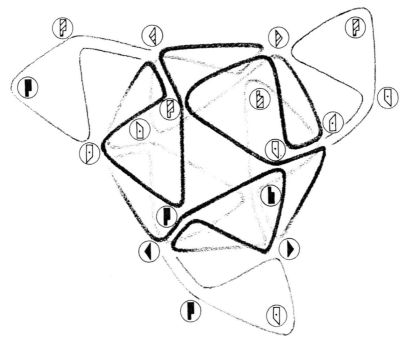

FIG. 44a.—*Process of spreading an uninterrupted surface-line of an icosahedron on a plane*
(stage 1).

in music can be traced here and it seems that between the harmonic life of
music and that of dance there is not only a superficial resemblance but a
structural congruity.

Music originates from rhythmical movement of the body and musical
harmony is surely a child of ancient trace-form knowledge as it is possible to
recognise musical harmony in the structure of a dodecagon. Dodecagons
can be found in many books on the theory of music; virtually, they are surface-lines connecting in one continuous circuit the dimensional cross, spread
into one plane.

It is the task of future choreutic research to investigate these amazing
relationships. The result will give much more than an aesthetic satisfaction,
for the building of symbolic forms, with their dynamic transformations into
different planes and plastic shapes, is one of the most profound inventions
of man's imagination.

In such investigations the scaffolding of the kinesphere will be of greatest
assistance. Some remarks concerning the similarity between the order in the

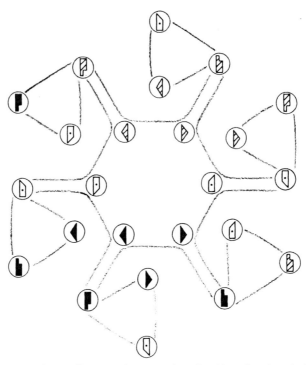

FIG. 44*b*.—*Process of spreading an uninterrupted surface-line of an icosahedron on a plane*
(stage 2).

scaffolding of the kinesphere and the scales of tones adopted in music may
be helpful in order to give an incentive for future investigations.

Dance uses seven fundamental cross-sections of space. These are the three
dimensions of an octahedron and the four diagonal cross-sections of a cube.
Music uses seven fundamental notes. If we arrange the seven cross-sections
of our natural orientation of space in such a manner that each of the three
dimensions is brought nearer to each of the four diagonal cross-sections, we
then have twelve cross-sections which are tempered, and therefore have
uniform distances between them (diameters). Between the seven fundamental notes of the modal system in music five others are placed. The
entire series of twelve notes, which are easily distinguished by the ear, are
slightly moderated in order to make the distance between each semi-tone
equal.

The series of distances between spatial cross-sections which the dancer uses to orientate himself form scales, and the series of musical notes also form scales. The "diaformic" scale which we propose to use in dance, consists of seven inclinations whose sequence divides into two unequal parts, one formed by three surface inclinations and the other by four. Five other surface inclinations form, together with the seven of the diaformic scale, a "chromatic" scale of twelve links (the standard scale).

The diatonic scale in music is made up of tones and semi-tones. It contains seven notes divided into two unequal parts. One part is formed by three notes, the other by four. Five other notes which fit between the notes of the diatonic scale make up the chromatic scale of twelve notes. The succession of elements which were chosen to form the scales is based upon a harmonic law (the law of circles), and constitute a series of octaves, fifths, fourths, thirds, and so on.

Moving through the surface-line standard scale, described in Chapter VII, and employing the diameters as connections between the various links, we achieve an arrangement which resembles that of the diatonic scale in music.

The trace-form in Fig. 45 shows the complete chain through which the arrangement of the "diaformic" scale is achieved. The diagram shows the

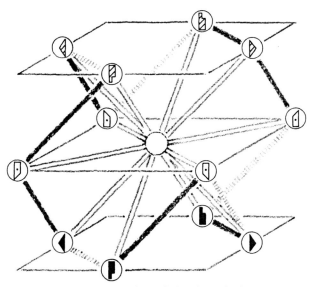

FIG. 45.—The "diaformic chain."

seven inclinations of the "diaformic" scale (black lines), together with the five inclinations indicating the links necessary for the formation of a chromatic scale (shaded lines).

The "diaformic chain" develops as follows:

◀ ··· ◗ ··· ◖ ··· ◗ ··· ◙ ··· ◗ ··· ▶ ··· ◖ ··· ◗ ··· ◖ ··· ◗ ··· ◗ ··· ◗ ··· ◀ ··· ◗

Each underlined link is an inclination of the standard scale. Joining every second one of this "diaformic chain" forms the sequence of the standard scale, thus:

◗ ··· ◗ ··· ◖ ··· ◖ ··· ▶ ··· ◗ ··· ◗ ··· ◀ ··· ◗ ··· ◙ ··· ◗ ··· ◖ ··· │◗

If we now investigate the placement of the seven inclinations of the diaformic scale within the standard scale the following result appears, showing a correspondence to the diatonic arrangement of musical tones.

The above underlined links:

◗ ··· ◗   ◀ ··· ◗
◗ ··· ◖   and   ◗ ··· ◙

lie beside each other without distance between, corresponding to the semi-tone intervals in the diatonic scale in music. The other links are each distanced from the following one by an inclination of the standard scale, which is not contained in the diaformic chain. The distance corresponds here to the whole step or tone intervals in the diatonic scale. As in music, where the diatonic sequence is partitioned by the half step or semi-tone intervals, through the absence of distances the choreutic chain is divided into two unequal parts, one formed by three inclinations and the other by four. Five other surface-lines, as already mentioned, are needed to complete the chromatic choreutic chain of twelve links, the standard scale.

(NOTE: there are also surface-line circuits of seven links in the icosahedron which have a similar unequal division. They, too, have a relationship to other surface-lines, which is reminiscent of the relationship of the twelve-note row of our modern musical system.)

Plastic models of seven-linked movable chains can be constructed which, when turned either by hand or in a mechanical manner, show by their progressive displacement spatial relationships in angles and distances. These correspond exactly to the sequences of the circle of fifths which constitute the backbone of the order of our musical tones. The borders of certain super-zones of the limbs of the body have the same formal rhythm showing identical harmonic relations.

Fig. 46 is a drawing of a model of a seven-linked chain movable in three-dimensional space.*

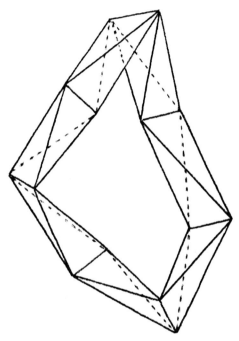

FIG. 46.—*Drawing of a three-dimensional model of a seven-link movable chain.*

The tonal relations mentioned above are primarily valid for Western music. Various scales of music belonging to other peoples and times also have analogies with sequences of spatial trace-forms.

European dance, based as it is on the ideal of formal beauty, follows the same general mathematical and geometrical laws as music. The different dance styles of exotic peoples, and those of past and primitive civilisations employ variations of the natural orientation in space. The relationships of inclinations in the kinesphere and the measurements of our bodily rotation,

* Invented by the author.

extensions and flexions (*see* Chapter X) have analogies with the relationships and measurements of acoustics.

The auditive orientation of music and its harmonic laws have come down to us through history and are derived from ancient researches and conventions. For example, the dances of the Middle Ages had forms which greatly resembled the forms of musical neums (neums are the oldest symbols of musical notation in our Western civilisation). The traditions of classical ballet have conserved the forms of *droit, ouvert, tortillé* and *rond* contained in these neums, and the five positions are relics which are comparable to the pentatonic scale.

Auditive orientation is based on physiological and anatomical laws governing the sense of hearing. Parallels between the construction of the ear and musical laws have been scientifically ascertained. Visual-tactile orientation is adapted to physiological and anatomic conditions of the moving human body and of the eye. Parallels between spatial orientation and the construction of our body have been scientifically ascertained, especially the functions of the eye, as reactions of our visual mechanism and the diffusion of light are closely linked.

Oscillations are the means of expression in the two arts, music and dance, but they have different forms (*cf.* the curves of Lissajou prototypes of oscillatory images of tones and their traces of harmonic movements). Psychologically, there is a remarkable parallelism between the modes (major and minor) in music and the two fundamental modes of the dance which are inherent in the attitudes of attack and defence. They express themselves in similar variations of fundamental scales.

Electro-magnetic oscillations which are inherent in matter seem to be similar to the oscillations forming our sense impressions of hearing, touching and seeing. The oscillations forming our motor-impulses may also be of the same form. All are subject to the same law of complication. This law, one part of which is the unfolding of agogic combinations (dynamism and tempo), is particularly clear in spatial harmony which is our basic experience in dance.

The parallel between the rhythm of music and dance is an accepted fact. The art of dancing has developed a conception of agogics which is founded on spatial ideas. Retardations and accelerations as well as the increase of intensity depend on directional intricacy. Between the harmonic components of music and those of dance there is not only an outward resemblance, but a structural congruity, which although hidden at first, can be investigated and verified, point by point. A real counterpoint can be developed in this way.

The knowledge of the harmonic interplay of trace-forms and their parts provides a new source for the composition of dances. The recording of dances, or dance notation, can become more than simple mnemonics. It can lead to constructive composition of trace-forms which are afterwards performed by the body.

Since the earliest periods of human civilisation there have been attempts to record movements which often paralleled the attempts to record music. The problem of this recording was always approached from two different points of view. If it is wished to record certain gestures only and their sequence, it is enough to portray the body of the dancer in the most important phases of its performance. A useful addition is the design of the path which the dancer follows on the floor.

This method of portrayal results in a kind of pictorial writing which is based on a realistic reproduction of the actual body of the dancer. It does not matter if the image is stylised, or sometimes mutilated, showing only individual parts of the body; the reproduction always remains pictorial, and deals only with the external aspect of movement. Many choreographers have approached the problem of recording movements from this angle only.

It is possible for the choreographer to create for his own use a system of mnemonics which helps him to remember a series of poses, but which would be unintelligible to an outsider without additional explanations. The portrayal of continuous dynamism, the essence of movement, demands another approach.

The preservation of artistic dance creations in a form which would enable posterity to study them and also to reproduce them, is one of the chief considerations which led to the study of choreutics and the invention of dance notation, but the problem has another side also. When we write down an idea, whether in words or in dance notation, we are compelled to clarify and simplify our first vague conception. The analysis necessitated by the process of recording unveils the inner as well as the outward nature of the movement.

It is, perhaps, a fantastic idea that there could be ideographic signs in a notation through which all people of the world could communicate. This, however, is not as extraordinary as it may seem. If we could write down "the thing," "the object," "the idea," "the action" in itself, and not its name only in an ephemeral national language, it would be possible for anybody of any nationality to comprehend the thing, the object, the idea, the action, and then to express it in their national idiom.

The words of language, giving names to objects and thoughts, conceivably sprang into being in remote times from movement impulses which were made audible. Thinking is certainly a kineto-dynamic process, and its trace-forms (presumably complicated shadow-forms, noticeable in free space lines) will one day be discovered.

The directional points of our customary orientation in space are abstractions of movements felt in the body (see Chapter I). In this respect they resemble other abstractions, namely those of actions made by the mind in thinking and in expressing thought through the words of language.

Movements contain different kinds of trace-forms. Geometric or mechanical ones may alternate with organic or natural biological forms. Another kind that can be observed is the personal, or free trace-form, which springs from the inner life of the individual. The regular trace-forms following the simple lines of the scaffolding can be represented mentally without great difficulty. The continually changing flow of free trace-forms, however, should be experienced by the body. Getting the "feel" of a movement gives real understanding of it. To construct phrases in choreutic language without vital experience, like making empty phrases in words about an event which has lost its significance, is obviously a break in the flow of life.

Movement in all the arts and in everyday work can be instigated by suggestions in movement notation, but it is not sufficient only to spell out the formal meaning of the symbols. To achieve an integral understanding, which is of the highest importance, a synthesis of a vital impulse with its performance by the body is indispensable. This performance need not be on a large scale. It can be so small that it is almost imperceptible to other people. It can, at times, approach pure meditation leaving the body apparently quiet. To learn the invisible performance of choreutic thought, so that it is felt in the body, is perhaps the finest achievement of the union of motion and emotion.

CHAPTER XII

Free Inclinations

MAN's movements create the most varied trace-forms quite freely in space, and in order to investigate their meaning and validity a notation is needed that makes it possible to record any desired inclination which may occur at any place, either inside or outside the kinesphere, without being bound to the points of the scaffolding. The future development of kinetography* must include the possibility of recording forms in free space which depends on an exact knowledge of choreutics, and this demands great powers of spatial imagination on the part of the notator. Mention of the problem of recording free space lines and inclinations must, however, not be omitted in a description of choreutics, since the conception of a notation capable of doing this is an old dream in this field of research.

Notating free space lines or free inclinations has various advantages. It is possible to describe not only trace-forms of the greatest variety of shape but also of placement in space. Our movements are sometimes very earthbound and stationary; at other times they seem to derive from and proceed to regions which cannot be reached by the body when rooted to the spot. Later on, perhaps, we shall be able to signify movements in free space through this basic contrast, namely, the earthbound tendencies of movements in scaffolded space when related to a centre, and the tendencies of movements independent of it when the vertical remains the only reference and inclinations are related to themselves. Tendencies towards infinite "smallness" and those towards infinite "largeness" could thus find a relatively simple description.

Furthermore, free space lines can be very useful in the notation of everyday movements, as well as of expressive movements in dance, and especially of details of movements which are not bound to definite and equilibrated

_____
* This is a term the author introduced for movement notation.

spatial harmonies. For a great number of modern dancers inclinations have a kind of individuality and they use them, mostly intuitively, with remarkable freedom.

The following practical results can be found which may prove valuable in this connection.

The twelve transversals:

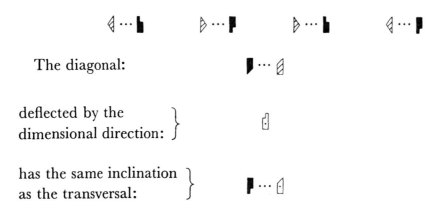

understood as deriving from the diagonals (*see* Chapter VII) show us that four of the twelve transversals are deflected by the dimension of height or length, four by the dimension of breadth, and four by the dimension of depth.

Those deflected by the dimension of depth are:

Those deflected by the dimension of breadth are:

Those deflected by the dimension of height are:

The diagonal:

deflected by the
dimensional direction: }

has the same inclination }
as the transversal:

but is centrally situated.

It is therefore possible to note the twelve transversals in the following way:

transversals:	diagonal directions:	deflected by dimensional directions:	simplified symbols of transversals:
▌⋯◁	◿	◹ (or f)	◿f
▙⋯◲	◺	◳ (or b, etc)	◺b
▌⋯◳	◺	◹	◺f
▙⋯◱	◿	◳	◿b
◁⋯◃	◺	◁	◺l
◲⋯▷	◿	▷	◿r
◳⋯▷	◿	▷	◿r
◱⋯◃	◺	◁	◺l
◃⋯▐	◢	▐	◢d
▷⋯▍	◣	▐	◣d
▷⋯▙	◣	▐	◣d
◃⋯▟	◢	▐	◢d

The following sequence of twelve transversals:

$$\natural \cdots \natural \cdots \blacktriangleright \cdots \natural \cdots \natural \cdots \blacktriangleleft \cdots$$

$$\natural \cdots \natural \cdots \blacktriangleleft \cdots \natural \cdots \natural \cdots \blacktriangleright \cdots |\natural$$

is parallel to the one mentioned above on page 126. The relationship of each of its transversals to the diagonals and dimensions can be established in the same way:

transversals:	diagonal directions:	deflected by dimensional directions:	simplified symbols of transversals:

It may be recalled that deflected diagonals go through the centre of the kinesphere, while an infinite number of parallel inclinations, including those of the transversals and the surface-lines of the scaffolding, do not go through the centre. To write these, we suggest the use of the simplified symbols in the above list. With these we can represent any free inclinations which are not bound to a centre, but occur anywhere in our surrounding space. Thus we can describe free lines, and free trace-forms of all kinds of shapes.

In free notation the dimensional and diametral directions, which are parallels anywhere in space to the dimensional and diametral crosses indicated in Chapter I, are signified by their endpoints only:

dimensional directions: diametral directions:

We can learn to mark any point of our surroundings with the help of a comprehensible symbol. The customary way of orientation (*see* Chapter I) provides us with 26 points on the surface of the normal kinesphere:

> 6 points from the dimensions
> 8 ,, ,, ,, diagonals
> 12 ,, ,, ,, diameters.

Inside this kinesphere we have the centre and 26 points of the restricted kinesphere (X). Outside we have another 26 points of the augmented one (M) (*see* Chapter IV).

All these points form a scaffolding of 79 points, and free inclinations can begin at any of these. These points are not directions or inclinations which in themselves involve movements but signal-points in the flow of movement and they are therefore put in parentheses in the following descriptions.

Below we give an example of a shape written with the symbols of free inclinations, indicating starting point, deviation and endpoint. In order to give the possibility of comparison the shape has been drawn to follow normal scaffolding lines (*see* Figs. 47 and 48).

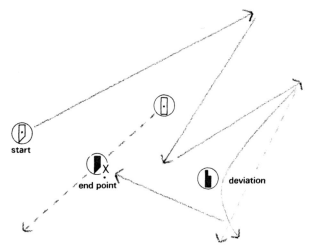

FIG. 47.—*A shape notated by symbols of free inclinations.*

starting point   deviation   endpoint.

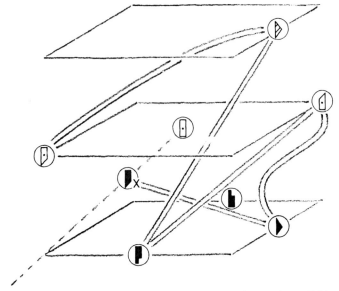

FIG. 48.—*The same shape as that shown in Fig. 47 in scaffold-writing.*

At first it will be necessary to fix some of the signal-points. Later it will be easy to follow a free space line when we write its starting point only. One of the most important questions is: how long is the spatial extension of the movement along the single inclination, if it is not marked by a stopping point?

If we know which sequences of inclinations are included in the scaffolding, it will always be clear whether or not the movement follows a surface-line or a transversal line. Paths of inclinations and dimensional directions not included in the scaffolding will appear very much shorter outside it, since they are not within easy reach. Those inside the scaffolding can pass close to the body and will therefore be longer if not stopped by a signal-point.

As already mentioned, dimensions and diameters anywhere in space are symbolised in free notation by their endpoints. The same is the case with the diagonals. They indicate movements parallel to those going through the centre of the scaffolding. For example:

is perpendicular upwards   (dimensional) ⎱
is right forwards horizontal (diametral)   ⎰ in relation to
is right forward high   (diagonal)   ⎱ a point anywhere
                                           ⎰ in space.

Example of free notation employing dimensions, diameters and diagonals:

dim. diam.   diag.

(▌) ⋯ ▨ₕ ⋯ ▌f ⋯ ▌ ⋯ ▨ ⋯ ▌d ⋯ ▨ ⋯(▨) ▌ᵣ ⋯ ▌b | (▌)

Awareness of bodily perspective (Chapter VIII) facilitates the understanding of the structure of space-lines which are not entirely built up by transversals, but do contain also other spatial elements. For instance: following the surface-line of the scaffolding from ♮ to ♮ and simultaneously taking several steps forward, we shall see that this flat inclination now extended into general space has changed its character of breadth to a character of depth. The inclination in the personal space, however, remains constant and the bodily feeling is still flat, although intellectual measurement shows that the path of the movement is now flowing. The inclination in the general space will approach the dimensional direction forward even more if the movement of the arm is accompanied by an increasing number of steps.

It is obvious that in practical movement and in dance the bodily feeling prevails. Therefore the symbols of notation must be related to personal space or the kinesphere. In Fig. 49 an attempt is made to analyse a free line.

(♮) starting point for the movement ▨ᵣ which is the surface-line ♮ ⋯ ♮ .

▨ₕ ⋯ is the continuation of the transversal ◀ ⋯ ♮ outside the scaffolding.

▌b ⋯ is a parallel to ♮ ⋯ ♮ very high outside the scaffolding.

▌d ⋯ is a parallel in counter direction to ▨ₕ ⋯ and leads to the scaffold-point (♮).

▨ ⋯ is the surface-line ♮ ⋯ ♮ .

(◀ₓ) causes a deviation towards the point (◀) of a small scaffolding during the execution of the following movement.

▨f ⋯ coming from (▨) the endpoint of the preceding movement is the surface-line ▨ ⋯ ♮ .

▌d ⋯ is the transversal ♮ ⋯ ▌ .

▌f ⋯ is the continuation of the transversal ♮ ⋯ ▌ outside the scaffolding.

▨ₕ ⋯ is a parallel to the transversal ◀ ⋯ ▨ outside the scaffolding.

(▨) is the endpoint of the movement.

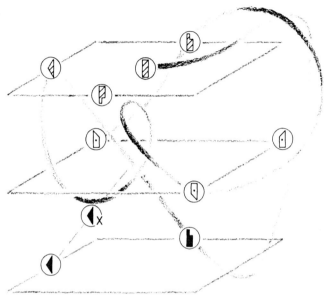

FIG. 49.—*An attempt to analyse a free line.*

Dynamospheric nuances can also be expressed by free notation. Actually, dynamospheric scales always evolve around free inclinations in the sense that they never have a precise place in three-dimensional space. They work, as we know, within the movements visible in the three dimensions, and are symbolised by diagonals around which they evolve like fluid shadows.

The way we discriminated between different trace-forms was by proceeding from single points to single rays and circular curves. Certain natural standard scales, at first described as going from point to point, are in reality built up from rays or inclinations. A further complication was the band-like trace-form which we encountered when dealing with the lemniscates and other indefinite shadow-forms.

Free notation employs symbols for inclinations, avoiding fixing them between points in the scaffolding as much as possible. The image of trace-forms becomes more fluid and we approach the irregularity of shadow-forms. Free lines and the forms built up by them can be understood as a kind of deformation of the scaffold-lines and forms. Thus we can say that the scaffold-lines are regular crystallisations of free forms which appear in the infinite number of possible movements. We can also understand the deformations as results of dynamospheric influences on regular scaffold-lines. This play between regular scaffold-lines and irregular free lines gives a hint as to the possibility of ordering and analysing the mental-emotional expression manifest in our movements.*

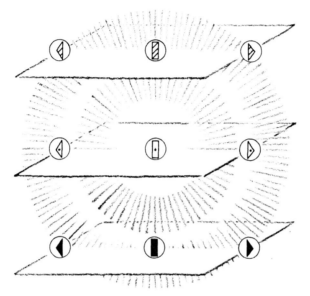

Fig. 50.—*A sequence of radial lines resulting in circles of admiration (implying adoration, awe, resignation, disappointment).*

left arm and hand: | ( ) ... ( ) ... ( ) ... ( ) ... ( ) ...
right arm and hand: | ( ) ... ( ) ... ( ) ... ( ) ... ( ) ...
or in reverse direction.

The dynamospheric standard scale developed in Chapter VI is written essentially by means of pure diagonals as axes for shadow forms. Dimensional axial sequences give the opportunity of describing a less active and more meditative kind of inner attitude. Movement or gestures of admiration, benediction or submission (*see* Figs. 50–52), for instance, appear free from such affective excitements as described in Chapter VI.

* In connection with his further explorations of dynamospheric influences (or effort) on movement Laban developed his "Effort notation." This is a means by which the nature of the control of exertion in space and time can be described.

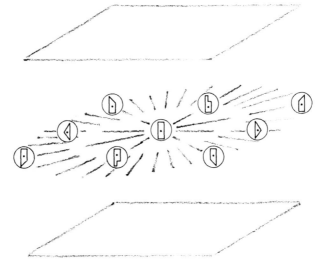

FIG. 51.—*A sequence of radial lines resulting in circles of benediction (implying blessing, welcome, humility, solitude).*

left hand and arm: | (⬚) ⬚ ... (⬚) ⬚ ... (⬚) ◁ ... (⬚) ⬚ ... (⬚) ⬚ ...
right hand and arm: | (⬚) ⬚ ... (⬚) ⬚ ... (⬚) ▷ ... (⬚) ⬚ ... (⬚) ⬚ ...
or in reverse direction.

Dimensional movements are combinations of several diagonal influences working together simultaneously. The diagonals paralyse each other and the result is an increased tendency to stability.

Almost all movements of worship introduced by priests of different religions are based on the simultaneous appearance of groups of action moods and become visible in trace-forms surrounding the dimensions. They are, in reality, not expressions of pure emotions, but of emotions mixed with reflective meditation and contemplation, thus they seem to connect the emotional world with the intellectual world—*seem*, because there is no obvious boundary between these two worlds.

We make artificial boundaries interrupting the real flow of movement only for the sake of analysis. If we understand this fact, analysis, as it is employed in the preceding descriptions of movement, can be most useful. The image given through analytical symbols, and revivified through personal experience, will thus be the source of advantages to be gained through the study of movement and the conscious enjoyment of it.

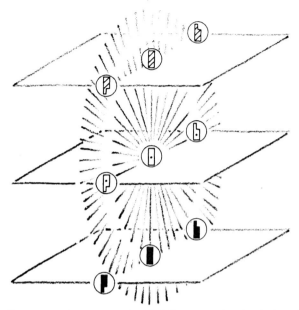

FIG. 52.—*A sequence of radial lines resulting in circles of submission (implying domination, obedience, devotion, pride, command).*

both arms or one: | ( ) ... ( ) ... ( ) ... ( ) ... ( ) ...
both arms or one: | ( ) ... ( ) ... ( ) ... ( ) ... ( ) ...
or in reverse direction.

With the three circles described above we return to our point of departure in Chapter I, the three dimensions, thus completing a circuit. It may be remembered that our first description of spatial orientation was based on an interpretation of bodily functions, which in the traditional art of dancing is derived from the five positions of the feet.

If we observe movement not only from the bodily perspective or from the intellectual conception of space-time orientation, but also from the threefold aspect representing the differing attitudes of individual personalities as suggested in the introduction, a new view and a new practice of our subject will arise.

The deductions made in these chapters may offer a basis for the development of a new aspect of space and movement. This has been indicated here, but the immense domain of this world is yet to be explored and an exhaustive research and description demand the collaboration of generations still to come.

One thing is certain. We can learn to read the evolutions of our movements and actions like a script as soon as we have acquired a certain degree of choreutic motor-experience, which includes practical experience of the significance of the different shapes and configurations stemming from our inner life.

Space-time configurations unfold in a flower-like manner; they swallow and engender formations; they wither and die and are reborn often filled with entirely unexpected inner and outer potentialities. Together with the dynamic rhythm with which the flowing energy drives along their tracks they constitute the vehicle of the language of movement.

PART II

Rudiments of Space-movement

This part is intended to supplement Part I rather than to develop it. As a guide to the basic essentials for the practice of spatial harmony in movement it has been given a different treatment so that the division into Sections with full descriptive under-headings may help the reader to survey at a glance the structure of the whole.

Division of Space through the Moving Body

IN Part I we have seen how we arrived at a conception of the kinesphere through the consideration of our moving body and how this spheric form is simplified by man's cubic conception of space (*see* Chapter II). The order within a cube—when looked upon purely as a space form without relationship to the body or its uses—is easily comprehended because of the right angles and equal edges. If we relate our moving body to this order we shall at first meet with some difficulties. Let us imagine that we are standing inside a cube whose corner points are within easy reach when we extend our arms and legs into the diagonal directions which we associate with the cube (Fig. 53).

1. THE THREE DIMENSIONS OF HEIGHT, DEPTH AND BREADTH

The up-down dimension

If, from our position within the cube, we now lift the right arm vertically as high as possible we shall find that:

(*a*) our movement has, so to speak, pierced the upper plane of the cube and reached a point beyond its boundaries;

(*b*) one side of our body has remained completely inactive and had no participation in the feeling of lifting upward;

(*c*) the weight of the body has been shifted to the right leg (Fig. 54).

However, if we transfer the weight onto our left leg, still stretching our right arm upwards, we can clearly feel a tension diagonal across the body, from the "high" of the outstretched right arm to the "deep" of the supporting left leg.

Only if we stretch both arms upwards and distribute the weight between the two feet, when a little apart, do we experience the feeling of a really

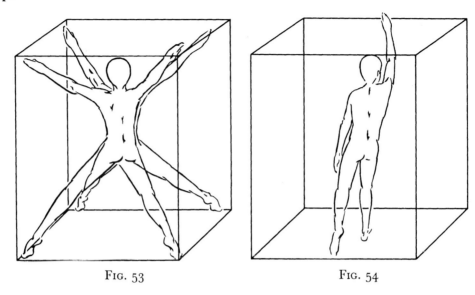

FIG. 53   FIG. 54

high-deep tension throughout the whole body. A split of the one-dimensional up-down extension has occurred; a spreading towards right and left thus produces a two-dimensional, plane-like tension (Fig. 55a).

The forward-backward dimension

Let us lift one arm forward and reach into that direction as far as we can. As a natural consequence, we may observe that the upper part of the body leans forward a good deal, while one leg tends to move into the opposite direction, backwards, somewhat off the floor. We notice that in order to make full use of the dimension (forward-backward) the body again enlists the help of an additional dimension (high-deep). Another possibility of experiencing a movement forward or backward is to stretch an arm and a leg simultaneously into either of these directions. The arm will naturally move forward or backward at a higher level than the leg. A split of the one-dimensional forward-backward extension has occurred; a spreading towards upward and downward thus produces a two-dimensional plane-like tension (Fig. 55b). (The introduction of a right and left division of the forward-backward dimension would not be so suitable, because the obvious turning forward—or backward—of one side when extending a limb as far as possible into this dimension is not as decisive as the forward or backward bending of the spine.)

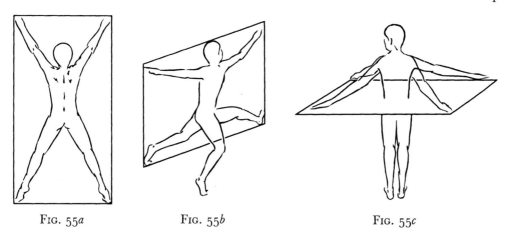

FIG. 55a   FIG. 55b   FIG. 55c

The right-left dimension

Let us step to the right first with the right foot and then with the left. If we do not wish to deviate from the purely sideways direction, it will only be possible for the left foot to step next to the right one, bringing the feet together, that is into the first position. In order to move the left leg to its opposite side, we have to change the pathway and cross either in front of or behind the right leg, thus enlisting once again the help of a second dimension (forward-backward). Similarly, we deviate the pathway of a sideways movement of an arm to its opposite side by crossing either in front of or behind the body. A split of the one dimensional right-left extension has occurred; a spreading forward and backward thus produces a two-dimensional plane-like tension (Fig. 55c). (If we led the arm across to the other side by moving it over the head we should feel this as a reaching up rather than as a moving to the other side.)

Planes in the three dimensions

We therefore see that the dimensions are not felt by the body as lines but as planes, namely:

    the high-deep dimension is extended right and left,
    the forward-backward dimension is extended high and deep,
    the right-left dimension is extended forward and backward.

Whilst the human body is not capable of making a purely one-dimensional movement, it can move, although in a rather restricted and hampered way, in the above mentioned planes.

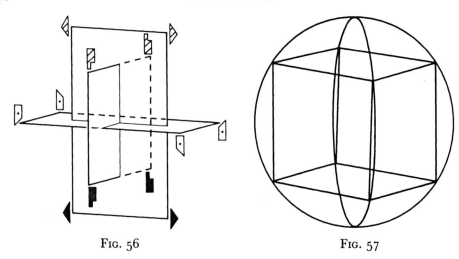

FIG. 56   FIG. 57

Fig. 56 shows the three dimensional planes intersecting one another.

By establishing the dimensional planes through the moving body, we arrive at a division of space, which no longer coincides with cubic space, a system which formed the basis for our space-orientation in the first place. We could, of course, visualise the dimensional cross extended into a system of planes within a cube, but the planes would then be squares. Looking at the above development of the dimensional planes which was arrived at from the one-dimensional extension we can see that these planes cannot be squares since one dimension was always the primary one, for instance, high-deep, to which another was added as a secondary one of less importance, in this case the right-left dimension. Therefore, the planes which the body feels as dimensional orientation are rectangles (*see* Chapter X).

2. THE ICOSAHEDRON

Referring to the conception of our personal space as a sphere and imagining a cube inside this sphere, we shall find that the cube will touch it with its eight corner points, between which six equal square planes extend forming its faces (Fig. 57). If, however, we picture the three rectangular dimensional planes within the sphere we see that their twelve corner points (four points of each plane) touch the sphere (Fig. 58). Between these extend twenty equilateral triangles as boundary faces, thus forming an icosahedron. This provides far greater detail of orientation than the cube. A scaffolding has

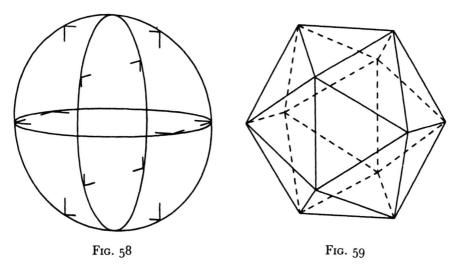

FIG. 58   FIG. 59

been created whose outer boundaries approaches a sphere much more than the less differentiated cube (Fig. 59).

This icosahedral scaffolding is divided in three ways by the dimensional planes. The high-deep-plane divides the movement space into an area in front and behind, the forward-backward plane divides right from left, and the right-left plane divides it into areas above and below (exactly as in a cube).

When the limbs move freely around the body it can be distinctly felt that the three dividing planes mark the turning points in the movement; e.g. an arc-like movement from forward to backward via high, rises until it meets the high-deep plane and then sinks to backward. Or an arc-like movement from left to right via forward advances forward to exactly in front of the body, meeting the forward-backward plane and from there recedes to the right side.

In considering man's natural way of moving we have so far stated that:

(a) purely one-dimensional movement never occurs;

(b) two-dimensional movement is possible but does not really correspond to the potential of human movement, because it is too bound and clumsy; its characteristic is stable.

Diagonals

We shall now consider the pure diagonal as the space-direction which stresses all three dimensions equally strongly. We may recall that in the

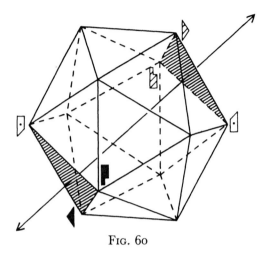

FIG. 60

cube it connected one corner with the opposite, crossing through the centre
(*see* Chapter I).

In the icosahedron it connects no corner points but penetrates the centre of
the triangles which are formed by the corner points of three dimensional planes.
For example, such a triangle is formed by the corner high-right of the high-
deep plane, forward-high of the forward-backward plane and right-forward of
the right-left plane. The opposite triangle is formed thus: deep-left of the high-
deep plane, backward-deep of the forward-backward plane and left-backward
of the right-left plane. A diagonal pierces the centre of these triangles (Fig.
60). As in the cube there are four pure diagonals in the icosahedron.

In contrast to the stabilising tendency of dimensional movement, movement
in diagonals is labile; in fact diagonals are the most labile of all space directions.
Our whole body can be moved into a purely diagonal direction only for a
fraction of a second; gravity forces us to seek a "foothold" in the stability
of one of the dimensionals. It is during a jump or a fall when we can momentarily move within one of these diagonals. One might even look upon the
diagonal as a force which induces movement.

Deflected directions

As another type of space direction in the cube, secondary deflections from
the diagonals and the dimensionals have been considered (*see* Chapter VII).
It was necessary to introduce them in order to define the division
of space in more detail. Now, when we consider directions in their

relationship to the moving body, we see that the deflected directions are those directions which, in contrast to the stable dimensions and to the labile diagonals, are used by the body most naturally and therefore the most frequently. In these deflected directions stability and lability complement each other in such a way that continuation of movement is possible through the diagonal element whilst the dimensional element retains its stabilising influence. The deflected directions in the icosahedron have a different degree of inclination from those in the cube (as the three-dimensional planes are not squares but rectangles), and they are easily felt because they correspond to the directions natural to the moving body.

For instance, if we imagine that we stand inside an icosahedron and extend the right arm into the diagonal direction right-high-forward and the left leg into the opposite direction left-deep-backward so that the tension between right hand and left foot follows the line of a pure diagonal, we can easily experience three different deflections. When we allow this diagonal to be deflected by the right-left dimension we shall observe, as we did in the cube, that the other two dimensions simultaneously lose influence and that the ends of the diagonal describe arcs in the kinesphere leading to the middle of the icosahedral surface-lines which lie between the points high-right and right-forward at the one end and at the other, between deep-left and left-backward (Fig. 61a).

If the same diagonal is influenced by the dimension up-down, one end of the diagonal will be deflected towards the middle of the surface-line which lies between the points high-right and forward-high and the other between deep-left and backward-deep (Fig. 61b). The third possibility of deflecting the same diagonal is towards forward-backward, when the ends of the diagonal in describing arcs in the kinesphere will eventually touch the middle of the surface-lines extending between the points forward-high and right-forward, and backward-high and left-backward (Fig. 61c). Each set of three surface-lines touched by either end of the deflected diagonal forms a triangle. (*See* Chapter VII: Fig. 26 illustrates the polar triangles surrounding the poles of the diagonal ◻ ... ◗ .)

The inclinations in the icosahedron are "tertiary deflections" from the diagonals and the dimensions and, similar to the "secondary deflections" as mentioned in Chapter VII, they have a flat, steep or flowing character as just demonstrated.

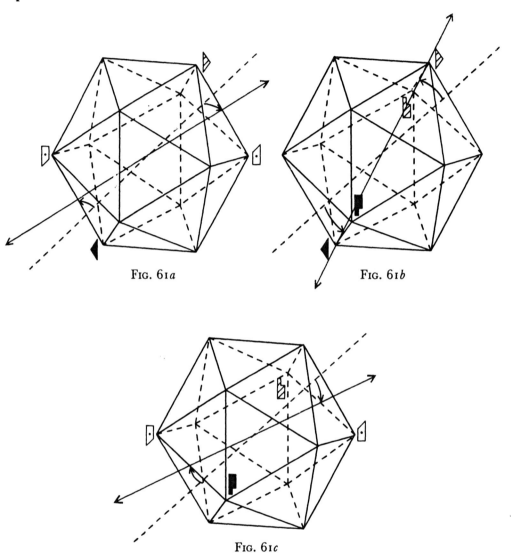

FIG. 61a

FIG. 61b

FIG. 61c

These three different characteristic deflections occur, of course, in all four diagonals resulting in twelve tertiary deflected diagonals.

Transposition of central directions

All the directions with which we have so far become acquainted intersect in the centre of our kinesphere. Observing man's natural way of moving, we however see that his movements do not often radiate from the centre of his body, but bypass it. His arms and legs, so to speak, loop around his

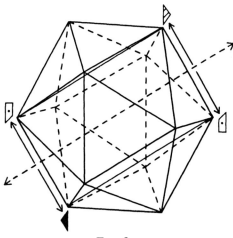

FIG. 62

centre. We therefore distinguish in our considerations of harmony of movement between "central" spatial lines meaning those which intersect in the
centre of the kinesphere and the body, and "non-central" lines, meaning
those which avoid the centre. Dimensional, diagonal and deflected directions
have the same directional value in both central and non-central movements;
there exist, therefore, spatial lines which lie parallel to the central ones (*see*
Chapter XII.)

Returning now to the inclinations within the icosahedral scaffolding we
find that we need only transpose the central inclinations in order to arrive
at those which are more natural to the body. Each central inclination can
be transposed in two ways according to the bodily structure, namely in
front of or behind the body (flat inclinations), or to the right or the left
(steep inclinations) or to above or below (flowing inclinations). (*See* Chapter
VII.)

Transversal inclinations

Thus "transversal inclinations" are created which now move between the
corner points of the aforementioned surface triangles rather than between
the middle of their edges. For instance, transpose the flat deviation of
the diagonal ⬧ ... ❚ in such ways that once it connects the points ◖ and ⬧
and then the points ◖ and ◀ in the icosahedral scaffolding (Fig. 62). It is
interesting to realise that the structure of the icosahedron with its corners
offers convenient points of orientation to the transposed inclinations in the

kinesphere. Each of these transposed inclinations connects two corner points of the icosahedron; i.e. the transversal deflections from the diagonal ▮ ... ▯ leading towards the lower end are:

flat   between corner points ▷ and ▯

  ,,   ,,   ,,   ,,   ◁ ,, ◀

steep   ,,   ,,   ,,   ▷ ,, ▮

  ,,   ,,   ,,   ,,   ▷ ,, ◀

flowing .   ,,   ,,   ,,   ◁ ,, ▮

  ,,   ,,   ,,   ,,   ▷ ,, ▯

When we consider the two triangles which these transversals connect we find that the diagonal ▯ ... ▮ passes through the centre of each.

The reader may be reminded of the fact that each dimension and each inclination has two directions (*see* Chapter I). This applies not only to the central dimensions, diagonals and diameters but also to all the non-central ones including transversal inclinations.

In dimensionsals and diagonals, movement occurs between extremes and it is therefore not so important from the bodily point of view in which direction the movement happens. With regard to transversal inclinations we find, however, an essential difference which depends on the direction in which these are performed. Let us consider, for instance, the steep ones of the diagonal ▯ ... ▮ , following the direction towards the upper end. The one connects the points ◀ (high-deep plane) and ▷ (forward-backward plane). The other, also in the direction upward, leads us from ▮ (forward-backward plane) to ▷ (high-deep plane). Both could also be performed in the opposite direction. Our body sense, however, finds it more comfortable, more pleasant, to move along the first mentioned inclination in the ascending direction, and along the second mentioned in a descending direction. The explanation for this may be that when travelling along the first inclination we start from the deepest point within our reach and the body feels it as a relief to move appreciably upwards, however, not to the extreme height; whilst moving in the opposite direction, starting from this height and moving to the deepest point, is more demanding. Exactly the opposite is the case with the other transversal. Having stretched to the highest possible point on the right, it is a relief to go steeply downwards again however, not to the utmost extreme. It is more demanding to move in the opposite direction, when starting not from the deepest possible point but leading to the highest. Therefore steep transversals will have their starting points in the high-deep plane (Fig. 63).

It is similar with the other types of transversals. The flat inclinations will have their starting points in the right-left plane, so that they can occur as a compensation to the extreme sideways tension, and the flowing inclinations will be most satisfactorily felt when leading away from the forward-backward plane. Which direction of an inclination we follow will, therefore, be determined by its starting point on a dimensional plane. We meet for the first time the fact that the compensation of extremes is of great importance for the flow of movement. We shall refer to this again and again as it is an interesting factor which we can observe in harmonious movement, namely, that the impulse to move is often more influenced by what happened before than by what is to come, or, in other words, the movement-impulse springs rather from reaction than from a desire for action.

The starting points of all transversals looping around the body centre are always in the corners of a dimensional plane. Two inclinations of the same character have a common starting point. (Fig. 64*a* shows two steep inclinations starting from each corner of the high-deep plane. Fig. 64*b* shows two flat inclinations starting from each corner of the right-left plane. Fig. 64*c* shows two flowing inclinations starting from each corner of the forward-

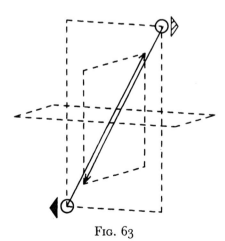

FIG. 63

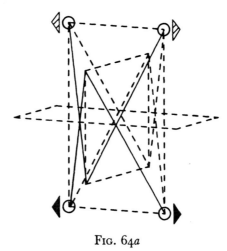

FIG. 64*a*

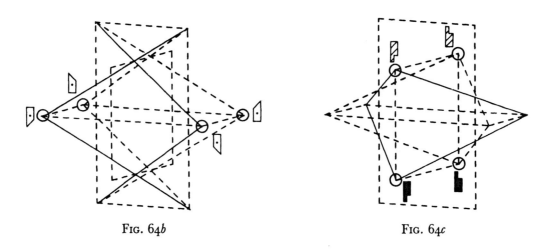

FIG. 64*b*   FIG. 64*c*

backward plane.) Since each dimensional plane divides the kinesphere into two halves (see above) each of these two inclinations leads into the opposite half, thus introducing a new tension.

For instance, the high-deep plane divides front from back. At each of its corners two inclinations will start, one leading its steep pathway forward and the other backward. Since the high-deep plane spreads between right and left, movements starting in the corners ♭ and ▶ will also lead somewhat to the left whilst those starting ⁊ and ◀ will tend towards the right. This indicates that one of the steep transversals starting from the point high-right is deflected from the diagonal ⁊ ... ▮ and the other from ⁊ ... ▮. The steep transversals starting from ▶ are deflected, one from the diagonal ◀ ... ⁊ and the other from ◀ ... ⁊ (*see* Chapter XII).

Sequential Laws

1. FORMATION OF SCALES

Cycle of flat, steep, flowing

WE have seen that all transversals connect one dimensional plane with another (passing on the way the third one) in such a manner that their endpoints provide a directional stimulus for the next movement. Since all flat transversals end on the high-deep plane, i.e. in an extreme high or deep position, in natural progression, a steep inclination is bound to follow which finds its termination on the forward-backward plane. Here the body is tilted either far forward or backward and a compensatory movement which is given by a flowing inclination is therefore called for. This in turn ends on the right-left plane, bringing the body into a position of extreme openness or closedness which finds its dissolution in a movement along a flat inclination. In this way a natural order of succession is indicated consisting of flat, steep, flowing, flat, steep, flowing, and so on.

The question now arises as to how this cyclic change of inclinations can be further realised by the body. At each endpoint of a transversal we have the choice between two new ones. One of these always retains the same diagonal value of the previous inclination, whilst the other leads into a new diagonal.

All our movements depend on two natural tendencies; we may refer to one as the instinct for stability and to the other as the instinct for mobility. The instinct for stability is embedded in the weight of our body and becomes effective according to the physical law governing a pendulum. The instinct for mobility urges us to overcome this weight and is most active when applying the physical law of the oblique plane and the lever (see below). These two instincts tend to be in conflict with one another, but when co-ordinated they produce a feeling of harmony. Therefore the most harmonious movement sequences which we experience are those in which both these instincts are taken equally into consideration.

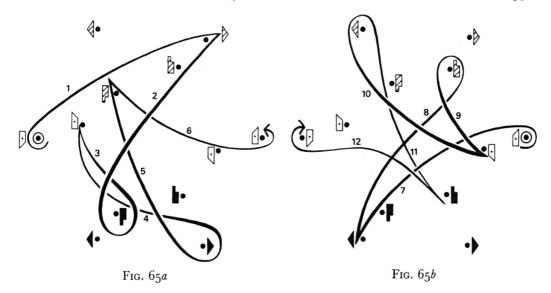

FIG. 65a   FIG. 65b

Transversal standard scales

The transversal standard scales in the icosahedron have the same structure as those in the cuboctahedron (*see* Chapter VII) and follow the
same sequential law, the only difference being the degree of their inclinations. These transversal sequences return to their point of departure after
twelve moves. (Fig. 65a shows the moves 1–6; and Fig. 65b the moves
7–12.)

It should be noted that all sequences, following this law, with their twelve
different transversals touch the twelve different corner points of the dimensional planes and are evenly spaced in the kinesphere. We may recall that
there are four such scales, each consisting of twelve transversal inclinations
(altogether, $4 \times 12 = 48$). This means that each inclination occurs twice within
each scale, first in one direction, and then in the counter-direction; the second
half of each scale is parallel to the first half (*see* Chapter VII).

If we perform the first movement of the scale, namely the flat deviation
of ◿ , and progress through the scale, we find that the seventh movement
is a flat deviation of the diagonal directions ▮ (same inclination, different
directions).

The second inclination is a steep deviation of ▮ , which has its parallel in
the eighth movement of the scale which is again a steep deviation of the
diagonal direction ◿ .

From this consideration it follows that each scale can contain only three
different diagonals.

	1st	diagonal=	1st	and	2nd	transversals
	2nd	,,	= 3rd	,,	4th	,,
	3rd	,,	= 5th	,,	6th	,,
again,	1st	,,	= 7th	,,	8th	,,
	2nd	,,	= 9th	,,	10th	,,
	3rd	,,	=11th	,,	12th	,,

Therefore in each scale one diagonal is missing.

What is the meaning of all this in terms of practical movement? And how
have we arrived at establishing the various facts?

It may be stressed that natural movement sequences existed long before
any theory about them was developed (*see* Chapter IV). In discovering
their lawful course these age-old movement sequences were evaluated and
established from the point of view of their twelve-partedness in a similar
manner to the way in which musical scales and other harmonic sequences
were established. Parts of these when used in freely created movement
sequences may lead to dance-like expression. But now we are concerned
with explaining their lawfulness and this we shall proceed to do.

2. CHANGE OF DIAGONAL AND ITS IMPORTANCE WITHIN THE SCALES (STEEPLE-VOLUTE)

The bi-partite rhythm of the diagonal directions and the tri-partite
rhythm of the inclinations (flat-steep-flowing) help us to analyse the transversal standard scales and to develop them movement-wise.

Let us perform one of the inner standard scales by taking as a movement-
unit always the two consecutive inclinations which are deflected from the
same diagonal. The result will be a series of restless rebounding movements. The whole movement sequence will appear sharp and pointed. We
may, therefore, call such inclinations which follow one another and are
deflected from the same diagonal "diagonal steeples." ("Diagonal steeples",
as distinct from "dimensional steeples," *see* page 166.)

Let us now take as a movement-unit those consecutive inclinations which
are deflected from two different diagonals. We shall notice that the

movements become smooth and fluent. This is because the inclinations do not follow one another in the sense of coming and going but continue into the second inclination along a curving arc-like path. We may call such movement-units "diagonal volutes." ("Diagonal volutes" as distinct from "dimensional volutes," *see* page 168.)

If the movement-units contained in the transversal standard scales were stressed instead of the cyclic change of flat, steep and flowing a rather restless feeling would be produced. One movement-unit would be "steeple-volute," the next "volute-steeple" and this, together with the inherent tri-partite rhythm, would interfere with the smooth continuation of the flux within the scales.

How does one now distinguish between the four transversal standard scales? We have already mentioned that there are three diagonals which play an active role in each scale and that the fourth is missing.

This missing diagonal is the decisive one in distinguishing one scale from another; it forms so to speak the backbone, the "axis" of the scale in question. All volutes of one scale circumvent the missing diagonal; e.g. the first volute steep-flowing (from ♭ via ▌ to ♮) circumvents the direct path ♭ to ♮ . This direct connection is a flat deflection of the missing diagonal ♮ ... ▌ in

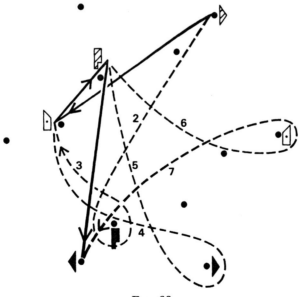

FIG. 66

reverse direction, i.e. it *goes to* the right-left plane, instead of *coming from* it. The second volute in the scale flat-steep (from ♮ via ▶ to ♯) circumvents the direct path between ♮ and ♯. This is again an inclination in reverse of the missing diagonal, but this time a flowing one. The third volute is flowing-flat (from ♭ via ♩ to ◀) and a circuitous arc around the direct path between ♭ and ◀, which is a steep deflection of the missing diagonal, again in the reverse. (Fig. 66 illustrates the above-mentioned three direct pathways with the volute circumvention of each.)

These three volutes (formed by six transversals) represent half the standard scale. Since one half is parallel to the other, the direct connections between the starting and endpoints of the next three volutes will also be parallel to those of the first half. Each volute is, therefore, a circuitous way around the missing diagonal and this diagonal forms the axis of the scale.

Structure of the transversal standard scales (A and B scales)

The following is a survey of the four transversal standard scales showing their structure and relationships.

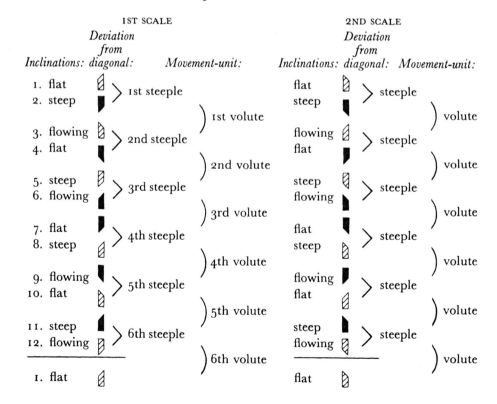

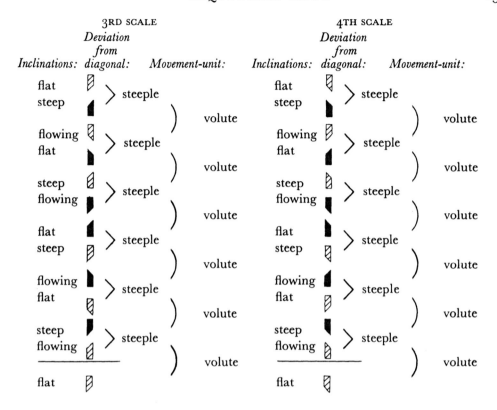

Comparing the four scales with one another we notice that the 1st and 2nd, as well as the 3rd and 4th, correspond with one another symmetrically (*see* Chapter VII). This can be clearly felt in the body, as the 1st and the 3rd scales contain movements essentially for the right side which are mirrored by the left in the movements of the 2nd and the 4th scales. For this reason we call the 1st and 2nd scales right and left A-Scale, and the 3rd and 4th scales right and left B-Scale. If we now take the two A-Scales as a unit containing 24 transversals, we see that they do not represent 24 different inclinations, but only 20. This is because the 1st inclination of the right scale is identical to the 10th of the left, the right 4th to the left 7th, the right 7th to the left 4th, and the right 10th to the left 1st. The right-left symmetry causes the flat inclinations, which cross from one side to the other, to exchange their identity in the two scales.

From now on we may refer to the *inclinations* of the right A-Scale (RA) by the symbols 1, 2, 3 etc. to 12, and to those of the left A-Scale (LA) by L1, L2, L3 etc. to L12.

When investigating the B-Scales we find that the inclinations contained are, though in different order, the same as in the A-Scales with the exception of the flat which have been replaced by four new ones. These are the inclinations connecting the points:

$$⌐|\text{ to }|⌐ \text{ (parallel to) } |⌐ \text{ to }▶$$
$$|⌐ \text{ to }◀ \text{ (parallel to) } ⌐| \text{ to }♭$$

The first pair of parallels are movements essentially for the left side of the body, and the second pair for the right side. The symbols "∞"* and "o"* have been added to the previous ones, 1 to 12, in order to signify these new inclinations: L∞ *(left infinity) for ⌐| to |⌐; Lo (left nought) for |⌐ to ▶; o (nought) for |⌐ to ◀; ∞ (infinity) for ⌐| to ♭. Like the flat inclinations of the A-Scales, all the new inclinations occur in each of the two B-Scales (RB and LB). Added to the previously established 20 inclinations of the A-Scales they bring the numbers of transversals possible in the icosahedral scaffolding up to 24 (*see* Chapter VII).

Expressive character of the transversal standard scales

Leaving these purely theoretical considerations concerning the structure of the scales, let us now look at the movement content. It has already been mentioned that each scale has its axis which is, so to speak, its backbone. This is valid beyond pure theory because the "missing diagonal" is decisive for the expressive character of the scale. For instance, in the right A-Scale the diagonal ∅ ... ▌ is missing. This is the diagonal in which, when leading with the right side of the body, strength can best be exerted, whilst the other three diagonals tend to hinder forceful movement of the right limbs in one way or another. This means, that the "strongest diagonal" is missing in the right A-Scale; consequently, a deficiency of natural vigour is noticeable in the movements within this scale; its character tends to the soft and moderate. In the left A-Scale the corresponding missing diagonal is ∅ ... ◀ which encourages energetic action of the left side.

The missing diagonal in RB is ♭ ... ▌, and in LB ∅ ... ▌. Each of these diagonals seems to promote a gentle quality of movement of the corresponding

* The symbols ∞ and o were chosen for convenience and have no mathematical or philosophic significance in this context.

body side. The B-Scales have, therefore, a much more active character than the A-Scales. This difference of expressive quality in the A- and B-Scales which is conditioned by the spatial emplacement of the movements may, in training, be aided by particular accompanying step patterns and rhythms.

For instance, when swinging through volutes of the A-Scales we might accompany the first inclination of each volute by a parallel leg gesture on the active side of the body, and the second by a step of the same leg in the direction of the final goal:

$$2 \text{ (with gesture)} - 3 \text{ with step}$$
$$4 \text{ (}\quad\text{,,}\quad\text{,,}\quad\text{)} - 5 \quad\text{,,}\quad\quad\text{,,}$$
$$6 \text{ (}\quad\text{,,}\quad\text{,,}\quad\text{)} - 7 \quad\text{,,}\quad\quad\text{,,}$$
$$\text{etc.}$$

Because the arm and leg on the same side follow parallel trace-forms the movement of the whole body has an easy and smooth flow. Correspondingly, in order to emphasise the virile character of the B-Scales, we bring the upper part of the body into strong opposition to the step-patterns. For instance, while the upper body takes the first inclination of the volutes, the steps should already be directed towards the end of the second, resulting in a counter-tension which is resolved only as the upper part completes the whole trace-form.

This kind of elaboration of these two scales may seem somewhat arbitrary, but it is based on the movement expression arising from spatial considerations. If we were to perform the A-Scales according to the principles of the B-Scales we should not be able to bring out the same strong and impulsive expression as in the B-Scales, and vice versa, a B-Scale will not easily lend itself to smooth and flowing movements as does the A-Scale. Because of this we sometimes refer to the scales thus:

A=female scales (minor scales)
B=male scales (major scales)

In this connection we may remind the reader of two facts:

(a) that the first six inclinations of the A-Scale resemble the defence movements in fencing (see Chapters IV and VII), and

(b) that not only is there a symmetry of the right and left scales but that each scale has a symmetrical relationship to every other. It is easiest to comprehend the right-left symmetry of RA and LA and of RB and LB since our body too has this symmetrical structure, but we are not in the same way aware of the up-down and forward-backward symmetry. These symmetries exist however in space and the reader is here once more reminded of them.

Interrelationships of transversal standard scales

As explained, the *right-left symmetry* forms the relationship between

RA and LA
RB and LB

the left side scale being the mirror movements of the right with the forward-backward plane acting as the "mirror," or being turned half-way round its axis, which extends between right and left (half a somersault).

In the first part of this book (Chapter VII) the echo-form and the mirrored echo-form of a scale were also mentioned. These forms appear in the inter-relationship of the A- and B-Scales as follows.

The echo-form, achieved through half a turn around the up-down axis, is found in the *up-down symmetry* of:

RA and RB;
LA and LB.

This symmetry is related to the right-left plane (half a pivot turn).

The mirrored echo-form is related to the high-deep plane and represents the *forward-backward symmetry*. It is the outcome of a half turn around the forward-backward axis (half a cartwheel turn). This relationship is found between:

RA and LB;
LA and RB.

All this can easily be recognised in movement by the fact that the right-left symmetrical scales have the flat transversals (1, 4, 7, 10) in common. The high-deep symmetrical scales have the steep transversals (2, 5, 8, 11) in common and the forward-backward symmetrical scales the flowing transversals (3, 6, 9, 12).

These inclinations shared by two scales always appear in the counterpart in opposite order:

$$\left(\tbinom{1}{L_{10}}\right)\ \tbinom{2}{L_9}\ \tbinom{3}{L_8}\ \left(\tbinom{4}{L_7}\right)\ \tbinom{5}{L_6}\ \tbinom{6}{L_5}\ \left(\tbinom{7}{L_4}\right)\ \tbinom{8}{L_3}\ \tbinom{9}{L_2}\ \left(\tbinom{10}{L_1}\right)\ \tbinom{11}{L_{12}}\ \tbinom{12}{L_{11}}\ \begin{array}{l}\to RA\\ \leftarrow LA\end{array}\Big\}\ \text{Flat}$$

$$\tbinom{1}{L_3}\ \left(\tbinom{2}{2}\right)\ \tbinom{3}{\infty}\ \tbinom{4}{L_6}\ \left(\tbinom{5}{5}\right)\ \tbinom{6}{L_o}\ \tbinom{7}{L_9}\ \left(\tbinom{8}{8}\right)\ \tbinom{9}{0}\ \tbinom{10}{L_{12}}\ \left(\tbinom{11}{11}\right)\ \tbinom{12}{L_\infty}\ \begin{array}{l}\to RA\\ \leftarrow RB\end{array}\Big\}\ \text{Steep}$$

$$\tbinom{1}{L_{11}}\ \tbinom{2}{\infty}\ \left(\tbinom{3}{3}\right)\ \tbinom{4}{L_2}\ \tbinom{5}{L_\infty}\ \left(\tbinom{6}{6}\right)\ \tbinom{7}{L_5}\ \tbinom{8}{0}\ \left(\tbinom{9}{9}\right)\ \tbinom{10}{L_8}\ \tbinom{11}{L_o}\ \left(\tbinom{12}{12}\right)\ \begin{array}{l}\to RA\\ \leftarrow LB\end{array}\Big\}\ \text{Flowing}$$

Vol-links

It has already been said that the missing diagonal of each scale has to be regarded as its "axis." In movement the individual inclinations of the axis occur when each volute is repeated. The link between the ending and starting points of a volute is an inclination of the axis, and we call it a *vol-link* (Fig. 66).

The six vol-links of the volutes of the RA scale are:

Volute		Vol-link	
	2 – 3	"	∞
" (L7) or	4 – 5	"	L6
"	6 – 7 or (L4)	"	L5
"	8 – 9	"	0
" (L1) or	10 – 11	"	L12
"	12 – 1 or (L10)	"	L11

of the LA Volutes:

Volute		Vol-link	
	L2 – L3	"	L∞
" (7) or	L4 – L5	"	6
"	L6 – L7 or (4)	"	5
"	L8 – L9	"	Lo
" (1) or	L10 – L11 or (10)	"	12
"	L12 – L1 or (10)	"	11

of the RB Volutes:

Volute	$0 - 8$	Vol-link	9
,,	$L9 - Lo$	,,	L8
,,	$5 - L6$	,,	4 or (L7)
,,	$\infty - 2$	,,	3
,,	$L3 - L\infty$	,,	L2
,,	$11 - L12$	,,	10 or (L1)

of the LB Volutes:

Volute	$Lo - L8$	Vol-link	L9
,,	$9 - 0$	,,	8
,,	$L5 - 6$	,,	L4 or (7)
,,	$L\infty - L2$	,,	L3
,,	$3 - \infty$	,,	2
,,	$L11 - 12$	,,	L10 or (1)

(NOTE: attention should be drawn to the particular volute which is given here as the first for the B-Scales. A convention has arisen to start the B-Scales in this manner because of a bodily feeling for balance in a commencing or concluding position.)

Axis-scales

The vol-links of each scale can be united in reverse order in one movement sequence, and this forms the so-called *axis-scales*.

Axis RA: $L11 - L12 - 0 - L5 - L6 - \infty$

,, LA: $11 - 12 - Lo - 5 - 6 - L\infty$

,, RB: $9 - 10 - L2 - 3 - 4 - L8$

,, LB: $L9 - L10 - 2 - L3 - L4 - 8$

Fig. 67a shows the scale of RA axis, and Fig. 67b that of RB axis.

Each axis-scale comprises all the six deflections of one diagonal. The four axis scales together, therefore, comprise all 24 inclinations, brought together in the order of their diagonal value. The movement produced by each axis is of a swaying, swinging kind.

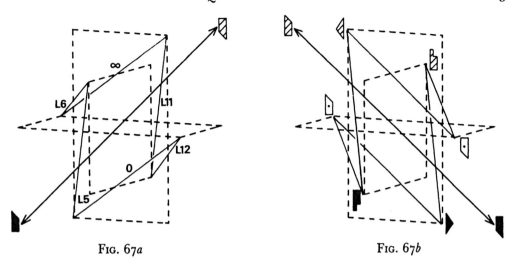

FIG. 67a   FIG. 67b

3. SEQUENCES OF TRANSVERSALS LEADING TO CONFIGURATIONS OTHER THAN SCALES

The four transversal standard scales and the four axis scales are the only scale-like configuration which result from assembling the 24 transversals in a harmonic order. Yet there are a number of other configurations which occur in movement again and again and which are formed by transversal inclinations. They have, however, no scale character. Of these the *three-rings* will be mentioned first.

Transversal three-rings

We call a volute a three-ring when, together with its vol-link, it forms a movement-unit, a circle consisting of three equally stressed sections. Looking at these three sections we notice that the three transversals contained are flat, steep and flowing inclinations, and that each of these three inclinations belongs to a different diagonal. The fourth diagonal is missing and forms its axis. In other words the three-ring moves around the fourth diagonal, which penetrates vertically the centre of the three-ring plane.

One might conclude that 24 three-rings would arise out of 24 volutes (six volutes in four scales). This is not the case by any means, but we find that two three-rings encircle each of the four diagonals, and that these eight three-rings contain all volutes. In analysing the three-ring $2 - 3 - \infty$ we shall see that it contains the following three volutes:

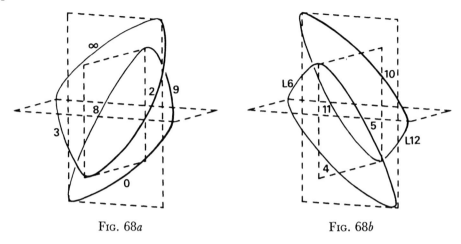

FIG. 68a   FIG. 68b

from RA Volute: 2 – 3 (Vol-link: ∞)
   „   RB   „   ∞ – 2 („   3)
   „   LB   „   3 – ∞ („   2)

Three-ring 8 – 9 – 0 (illustrated in Fig. 68a) contains:

from RA Volute: 8 – 9 (Vol-link: o)
   „   RB   „   0 – 8 („   9)
   „   LB   „   9 – o („   8)

Correspondingly on the left side.
Three-ring 4 – 5 – L6 (illustrated in Fig. 68b) contains:

from RA Volute: 4 – 5   (Vol-link: L6)
   „   LA   „   L6 – L7 or (4) („   5)
   „   RB   „   5 – L6   („   4)

Three-ring 10 – 11 – L12 contains:

from RA Volute: 10 – 11   (Vol-link: L12)
   „   LA   „   L12 – L1 or (10) („   11)
   „   RB   „   11 – L12   („   10)

Correspondingly on the left side.

Thus the manifoldness of the volutes is suddenly reduced to eight circular configurations which contain all the possibilities arising from the four twelve-link scales. These provide simple themes from which harmonious movement sequences and variations can be developed, especially if the scale characteristics of each volute are brought out.

Snakes

Other simple configurations are the *snakes* (so-called because they have a serpentine trace-form) which represent parts of the transversal scales, and consist of one volute and the following steeple. As the three-rings, they also contain a flat, a steep, and a flowing inclination but, instead of encircling a diagonal, they always circumvent with three movements a transversal dimension; for instance in the trace-form: 2 – 3 – 4 the change is made from high to deep on the right (♭ to ▶) which is a transversal dimension but the actual trace-form follows a serpentine path from ♭ ... ▮ ... ♮ ... ▶ . The snakes also frequently occur as elementary movement themes.

Shears

The next movement sequences to be mentioned are configurations also consisting of transversals only, which we call *shears*. In these, for the first time, we encounter inverted transversals, i.e. transversals taken in the reverse direction. This means that we no longer follow the most elementary laws, but begin to include some complications. The shears, therefore, appear rarely as independent movement-themes, but rather as links between two different scales. Expressively they have either a restraining (*ritardando*) or promoting (*accellerando*) influence on the flow of movement which has, so to speak, to be taken by storm in order to overcome the resistance presented by the inverted inclinations.

The shears consist of four transversals and always have a completely symmetrical structure; they can be considered from a central point on their trace-line from which inclinations of identical character travel in either direction, towards the beginning or towards the end of the line. We distinguish different kinds of shears according to the order in which steeples and volutes are combined. The central part of each of these movement units therefore consists of either two steep, two flowing or two flat inclinations. If

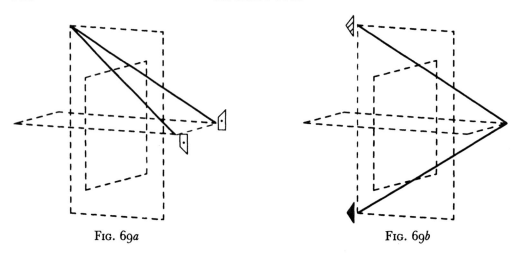

FIG. 69a   FIG. 69b

the starting and ending points of these two combined inclinations are
separated by a peripheral* dimension we speak of a dimensional steeple
(Fig. 69a). If, however, they are separated by a transversal dimension we
speak of a dimensional volute (Fig. 69b). The angles of the dimensional
steeples and volutes are the same as those of the diagonal steeples and
volutes.

Dimensional steeples are:

$$
\begin{array}{rll}
\text{Flat:} & 1 - \infty & \text{(inverted)} \\
& \text{L}1 - \text{L}\infty & \text{,,} \\
& 7 - 0 & \text{,,} \\
& \text{L}7 - \text{L}0 & \text{,,}
\end{array}
\Bigg\} \quad \text{(Fig. 70a)}
$$

$$
\begin{array}{rll}
\text{Steep:} & 2 - \text{L}2 & \text{(inverted)} \\
& 5 - \text{L}5 & \text{,,} \\
& 8 - \text{L}8 & \text{,,} \\
& 11 - \text{L}11 & \text{,,}
\end{array}
\Bigg\} \quad \text{(Fig. 71a)}
$$

$$
\begin{array}{rll}
\text{Flowing:} & 3 - \text{L}6 & \text{,,} \\
& 12 - \text{L}9 & \text{,,} \\
& \text{L}3 - 6 & \text{,,} \\
& \text{L}12 - 9 & \text{,,}
\end{array}
\Bigg\} \quad \text{(Fig. 72a)}
$$

* "Peripheral" means that the movement follows a surface-line of the scaffolding (see
Chapter VII).

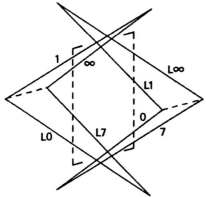

FIG. 70a

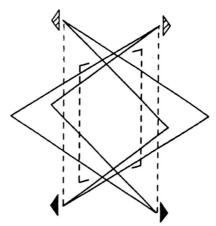

FIG. 70b

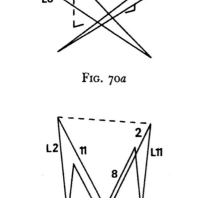

FIG. 71a

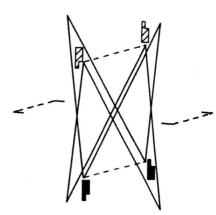

FIG. 71b

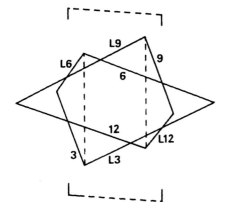

FIG. 72a

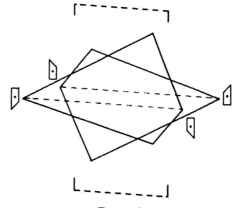

FIG. 72b

Dimensional steeples always include one inverted inclination, which is the *second* in the sequence, as seen above.

Dimensional volutes are:

Flat: (inverted) Lo – 1
,,   .0 – L1
,,   L∞ – 7   } (Fig. 70*b*)
,,   ∞ – L7

Steep: 2 – L11
,,   L2 – 11
,,   5 – L8   } (Fig. 71*b*)
,,   L5 – 8

Flowing: ,,   3 – L3
,,   6 – L6
,,   9 – L9   } (Fig. 72*b*)
,,   12 – L12

Dimensional volutes also include one inverted inclination, which is, however, the *first* in the sequence, as seen above.

The character of the shears is identified by the fact that a dimensional volute or a dimensional steeple forms the centre of the configuration. In addition, either a diagonal steeple or a diagonal volute appears as preparation and conclusion of the movement, so that we have the following variations of the shears:

small   shears: steeple, steeple, steeple
medium   ,,   : volute, steeple, volute
large   ,,   : steeple, volute, steeple
augmented ,,   : volute, volute, volute

EXAMPLES:

small shears (3rd & 4th   L9 – 1 – ∞ – L6
inclinations inverted):   1 – 2 – L2 – L1 (Fig. 73*a*)
                             L2 – 3 – L6 – L5, etc.

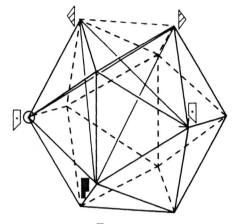

FIG. 73a

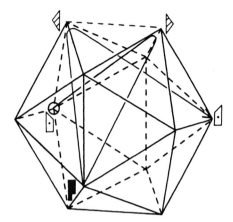

FIG. 73b

medium shears (3rd & 4th inclinations inverted):	$12 - 1 - \infty - 3$
	$\infty - 2 - L2 - L\infty$ (Fig. 73b)
	$2 - 3 - L6 - 5$
large shears (1st & 2nd inclinations inverted):	$5 - Lo - 1 - 2$ (Fig. 73c)
	$L3 - 2 - L11 - L12$
	$L7 - 3 - L3 - 7$
augmented shears (1st & 2nd inclinations inverted):	$L8 - Lo - L10 - L11$ (Fig. 73d)
	$3 - 2 - L11 - 12$
	$\infty - 3 - L3 - L\infty$

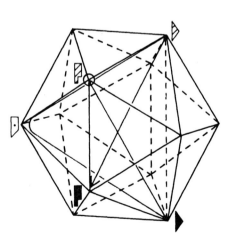

FIG. 73c

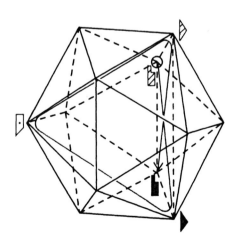

FIG. 73d

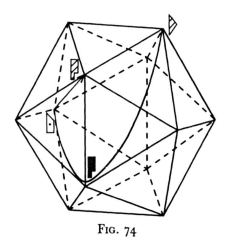

FIG. 74

Diminished three-rings

Inverted inclinations are also to be found in the *diminished three-rings*. These are trace-forms in which another deflection from the diagonal of the vol-link replaces the latter, forming a dimensional steeple relationship with the previous inclination. Instead of closing the circle the movement is thus drawn into a narrowing spiral.

For example, instead of the ring 2 – 3 being closed by ∞, 2 – 3 is followed by L6 inverted, thus spiralling towards 𝄮 (Fig. 74). Similarly:

4 – 5	instead of L6 follows	L5 inverted; spiralling towards ◀
6 – 7	,, ,, L5 ,,	o ,, ,, ,, 🯄
8 – 9	,, ,, o ,,	L12 ,, ,, ,, ▌
10 – 11	,, ,, L12 ,,	L11 ,, ,, ,, ▷
12 – 1	,, ,, L11 ,,	∞ ,, ,, ,, 🯅
o – 8	,, ,, 9 ,,	L8 ,, ,, ,, ▸
L9 – Lo	,, ,, L8 ,,	L7 ,, ,, ,, 🯅
5 – L6	,, ,, L7 ,,	3 ,, ,, ,, ▐
∞ – 2	,, ,, 3 ,,	L2 ,, ,, ,, ◁
L3 – L∞	,, ,, L2 ,,	10 ,, ,, ,, 🯄
11 – L12	,, ,, 10 ,,	9 ,, ,, ,, 🯅

The diminished three-rings are trace-forms which frequently occur in natural movement sequences and they often form transitions to new movement themes. (This aspect is further considered in a later section.)

Peripheral Movements

LET us now consider *peripheral directions*.

1. SINGLE DIRECTIONS

When our limbs are extended far away from the centre of the body our movements tend to become spheric; we move in an undefined sphere which constitutes our "kinesphere." Peripheral directions are the boundary lines of a scaffolding within it and they produce peripheral trace-lines which the body is just able to distinguish as having definite directional character. For reasons explained in other parts of this book the icosahedral shape is of prime importance in human movement and the peripheral directions to which we refer here are the surface edges of an icosahedron. There are thirty of these connecting the twelve corners of the dimensional planes. For instance from ♭ five such peripheral movements lead towards five directions: ⟨ ; ⟨ ; ♭ ; ⟨ ; ♮ (Fig. 75). Similarly five peripheral directions lead away from all other corners.

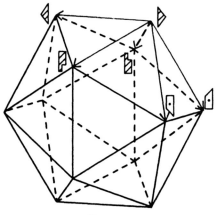

FIG. 75

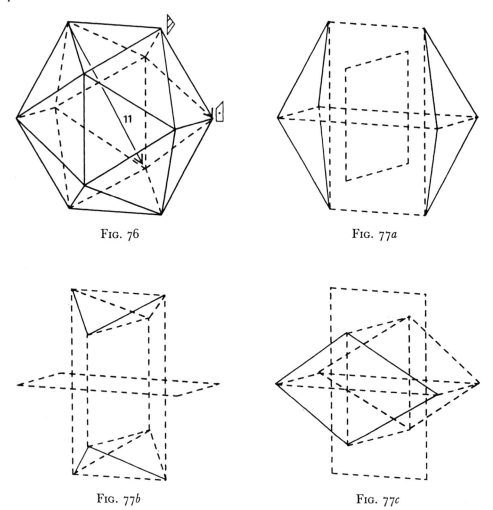

FIG. 76

FIG. 77a

FIG. 77b

FIG. 77c

Parallelism to transversals

Examining these peripheral movements we find they do not constitute new directional inclinations, but are the same as those of the transversals only transposed further away from the centre of the kinesphere. For instance, the peripheral movement from ♭ to ♮ is a steep deflection from the diagonal direction ◀, and is parallel to 11 (Fig. 76). The peripheral from ♭ to ♮ is also steep but deflected from the diagonal direction ▌. A steep peripheral inclination leads from ▶ to ♮; it is deflected from the diagonal direction ♯ and is therefore parallel to 8; likewise a steep peripheral rises from ▶ to ♮ which is parallel to L5. On the left side, correspondingly, starting from ◁ we find the peripheral inclinations parallel to L11 and L2, and from ◀ those parallel to L8 and 5. We may observe that the steep inclinations are again related to the high-deep plane by being grouped around it (Fig. 77*a*). Similarly, we find the flowing peripheral inclinations grouped around the forward-backward dimensional plane (Fig. 77*b*) and the flat ones around the right-left dimensional plane (Fig. 77*c*) as follows:

Fundamental location of peripherals

peripheral:	deflection:	diagonal direction:	transversal:
from ▯ to ▯	flowing	▯	parallel to L12
,, ▯ ,, ◁	,,	▯	,, ,, 12
,, ▯ ,, ▯	,,	▯	,, ,, L3
,, ▯ ,, ◁	,,	▯	,, ,, 3
,, ▮ ,, ▶	,,	▮	,, ,, 9
,, ▮ ,, ◀	,,	▮	,, ,, L9
,, ▮ ,, ▶	,,	◀	,, ,, 6
,, ▮ ,, ◀	,,	▮	,, ,, L6
,, ◁ ,, ▯	flat	▯	,, ,, L1 or 10
,, ◁ ,, ▮	,,	▮	,, ,, 0
,, ▯ ,, ▯	,,	▯	,, ,, 1 or L10
,, ▯ ,, ▮	,,	◀	,, ,, L0
,, ◁ ,, ▯	,,	▯	,, ,, L∞
,, ◁ ,, ▮	,,	▮	,, ,, 7 or L4
,, ▯ ,, ▯	,,	▯	,, ,, ∞
,, ▯ ,, ▮	,,	◀	,, ,, L7 or 4
,, ▶ ,, ◁	steep	◀	,, ,, 11
,, ▶ ,, ◁	,,	◀	,, ,, L2
,, ▶ ,, ◁	,,	▯	,, ,, 8
,, ▶ ,, ◁	,,	▯	,, ,, L5
,, ◁ ,, ▯	,,	▮	,, ,, L11
,, ◁ ,, ▯	,,	▮	,, ,, 2
,, ◀ ,, ▯	,,	▯	,, ,, L8
,, ◀ ,, ▯	,,	▯	,, ,, 5

It may be mentioned here that the peripheral inclinations have no fixed direction of movement. They are identified by the diagonal direction from

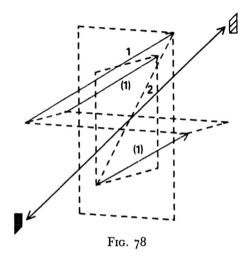

FIG. 78

which they are deflected, although the most natural way is produced when the movements compensate the extreme extension of the plane from which they start. The peripheral 11, for instance (*see* Fig. 76), which leads from ⟨to ⟨, is often used in the reverse direction, that is the direction of the transversal 5, and then it is also called 5. Therefore this peripheral can be referred to as 5 or 11 depending on the direction in which the movement has been performed. This rule applies to all peripherals.

In order to facilitate further orientation within the peripheral inclinations the following help is given. The two parallel transversals have two peripheral parallels, for instance:

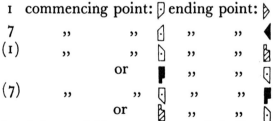

(NOTE: the ciphers within parentheses () indicate peripherals.)

The relationship of the transversal 1 with the peripheral (1) is to be found in the peripheral forward-backward dimension, of the right-left plane connecting ⟨with ⟨(Fig. 78). If a transversal is transposed along a peripheral dimension the inclination is not changed but it has become a peripheral. The other peripheral (1) (behind the body) occurs as a kind of rebound after a swing of the right arm along the transversal inclination 2 (Fig. 78). Both these movements, 2 and its rebound (1), belong to the same diagonal. Similarly, the transversal 7 is related to the peripheral (7), behind the body, through transposition along the peripheral forward-backward dimension of the right-left plane (⌐ ... ⌐). To the peripheral (7), in front of the body, it is related through the rebound following the transversal 8 with which it forms a steeple:

$$ ⌐\!\cdots\!◀\!\cdots\!⌐\!\cdots\!⌐ $$
$$ \;\;7\quad 8\quad (7) $$

The role played by these peripheral inclinations in free movement is greater than one might think, because arc-like movements, arising from the connection of certain peripheral inclinations is more congenial to the dancer than the line-like ones of the transversals. One often imagines oneself to be moving along transversals, when in fact one takes the peripheral deviations. It may be of interest to mention here that the peripherals are of great assistance in defining the shape of gathering and scattering curves produced by sequences of transversals (*see below*).

2. SEQUENCES OF PERIPHERALS ARISING FROM THE CIRCUMVENTION OF TRANSVERSALS

Let us recall the three-rings, as the first trace-form to which we might relate the peripherals. Each of them has the character of a "gathering circle" or a "scattering circle," (*see* Chapter V). The two three-rings around ⌐ ... ◀, 2 − 3 − ∞ and 8 − 9 − 0 are, when active with the right side of the body, definitely gathering circles whilst those around ⌐ ... ▶, 4 −5 − L6 and 10 − 11 − L12 are scattering ones.

Bearing this in mind, if we now swing, for instance, 2 − 3 − ∞, i.e. if we use less rigid movements (Fig. 79*a*), we shall perform arc-like pathways which we can analyse as follows:

the arc around   2   deviating toward ⌐ consists of: (L2) − (L4)
   „ „   „   3   „   „ ▶ „   „ (L6) − (L8)
   „ „   „   ∞   „   „ ⌐ „   „ (L10) − (L12)

13

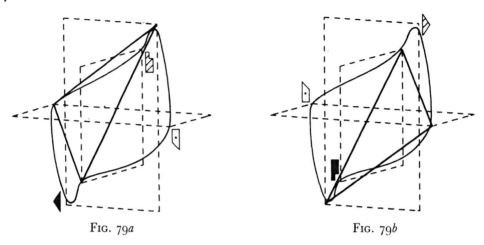

FIG. 79a   FIG. 79b

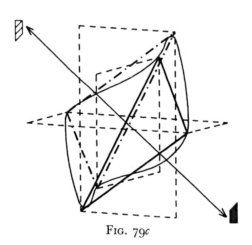

FIG. 79c

If we swing 8 – 9 – 0 as a large gathering circle (Fig. 79*b*), this can be analysed thus:

the arc around 8 deviating toward ◗ consists of: (L8) – (L10)

  ,,   ,,   ,,   9   ,,   ,,   ◗   ,,   ,, (L12) – (L2)

  ,,   ,,   ,,   0   ,,   ,,   ▮   ,,   ,, (L4) – (L6)

4 – 5 – L6 as a scattering circle appears like this:

the arc around 4 deviating toward ▌consists of: (Lo) – (9)

,, ,, ,, 5 ,, ,, ▯ ,, ,, (L5) – (L∞)

,, ,, ,, L6 ,, ,, ◪ ,, ,, (3) – (L11)

10 – 11 – L12, as a scattering circle, appears like this:

the arc around 10 deviating toward ◩consists of: (L∞) – (3)

,, ,, ,, 11 ,, ,, ▯ ,, ,, (L11) – (Lo)

,, ,, ,, L12 ,, ,, ▶ ,, ,, (9) – (L5)

We have, of course, corresponding results with the three-rings around the other two diagonals ◪ ... ▌ and ◩ ... ◀ when active with the left side of the body.

L2 – L3 – L∞ – is circumscribed by (2) – (4) – (6) – (8) – (10) – (12)

L8 – L9 – Lo – ,, ,, ,, ,, (8) – (10) – (12) – (2) – (4) – (6)

L4 – L5 – 6 – ,, ,, ,, ,, (0) – (L9) – (5) – (∞) – (L3) – (11)

L10 – L11 – 12 – ,, ,, ,, ,, (∞) – (L3) – (11) – (0) - – (L9) – (5)

When we now study the peripheral deviations of the two parallel three-rings we find that both are surrounded by the same peripheral circle which, so to speak, links them together. Therefore, when we move along the trace-form of a three-ring in a slinging manner a peripheral circle (consisting of six parts) which embraces also the three-ring parallel to it will result (Fig. 79c).

Girdle or equator scales

Here it may be mentioned that the configuration arising from the circumvention of a three-ring, being the largest circle around a diagonal, has been named *equator scale* or *girdle* (*see* Chapter VII). There are four equators, one around each missing diagonal of the four transversal standard scales which becomes its axis. The following table shows the scales to which the equators, with their two circumscribed three-rings, belong. Those inclinations of a scale which appear as peripherals in its girdle are indicated by italic figures in the next table.

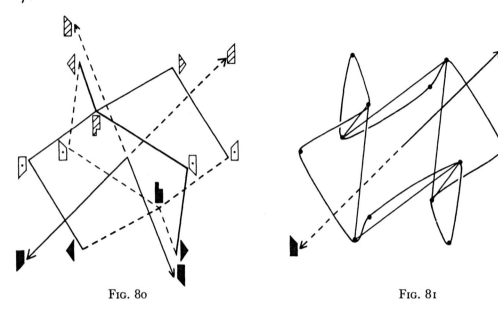

FIG. 80   FIG. 81

Three-ring:	*Equator:*	*Axis: Scale:*

$$
\left.\begin{matrix} 2-\ \ 3\ -\infty \\ 8-\ \ 9\ -\ o \end{matrix}\right\} \ (L2)-(L4)-(L6)-(L8)-(L10)-(L12)\ \diagdown\!\!...\blacktriangleleft\ LA
$$

$$
\left.\begin{matrix} L2-L3-L\infty \\ L8-L9-Lo \end{matrix}\right\} \ (2)-\ (4)\ -\ (6)\ -\ (8)\ -\ (10)\ -\ (12)\ \diagup\!\!...\blacktriangleright RA
$$

$$
\left.\begin{matrix} 4-\ \ 5\ -L6 \\ 10-11-L12 \end{matrix}\right\} (Lo)-\ (9)\ -(L5)-(L\infty)-\ (3)\ -(L11)\ \blacktriangledown\!\!...\diagup LB
$$

$$
\left.\begin{matrix} L4-L5-\ 6 \\ L10-L11-12 \end{matrix}\right\} \ (o)-(L9)-\ (5)\ -\ (\infty)-(L3)-\ (11)\ \blacktriangle\!\!...\diagdown RB
$$

(Fig. 80)

We can see that each girdle consists of the first inclination of the volutes contained in the scale to which it belongs:

>   RA: *2 – 3 – 4 – 5 – 6 – 7 – 8 – 9 – 10 – 11 – 12 – 1*
>   LA: correspondingly.
>   RB: *0 – 8 – L9 – Lo – 5 – L6 – ∞ – 2 – L3 – L∞ – 11 – L12*
>   LB: correspondingly.

We therefore find that a girdle represents the peripheral sequence of the first inclinations of the volutes.

Peripheral standard scales or primary scales

In the same way that the three-rings are easily circumvented so can the "cluster" be curved by peripheral deviations through freely slinging movements. Again we find harmonic relations with the transversal standard scales.

The resulting deviations of the RA cluster or axis scale (Fig. 81) are:

the arc around ∞ deviating toward ♮ consisting of: (1) – (L12)

  ,,   ,,   ,,   L11   ,,   ,,   ◖   ,,   ,,   (11) – (0)

  ,,   ,,   ,,   L12   ,,   ,,   ▶   ,,   ,,   (9) – (L5)

  ,,   ,,   ,,   0   ,,   ,,   ▮   ,,   ,,   (7) – (L6)

  ,,   ,,   ,,   L5   ,,   ,,   ▯   ,,   ,,   (5) – (∞)

  ,,   ,,   ,,   L6   ,,   ,,   ◁   ,,   ,,   (3) – (L11)

The deviations of the LA axis scale are:

the arc around L∞ deviating toward ♮ consisting of: (L1) – (12)

  ,,   ,,   ,,   11   ,,   ,,   ◗   ,,   ,,   (L11) – (L0)

  ,,   ,,   ,,   12   ,,   ,,   ◀   ,,   ,,   (L9) – (5)

  ,,   ,,   ,,   L0   ,,   ,,   ▮   ,,   ,,   (L7) – (6)

  ,,   ,,   ,,   5   ,,   ,,   ▯   ,,   ,,   (L5) – (L∞)

  ,,   ,,   ,,   6   ,,   ,,   ♭   ,,   ,,   (L3) – (11)

The deviations of the RB axis scale are:

the arc around 10 deviating toward ♮ consisting of: (L∞) – (3)

  ,,   ,,   ,,   L2   ,,   ,,   ▯   ,,   ,,   (2) – (4)

  ,,   ,,   ,,   3   ,,   ,,   ◀   ,,   ,,   (L6) – (L8)

  ,,   ,,   ,,   4   ,,   ,,   ▮   ,,   ,,   (L0) – (9)

  ,,   ,,   ,,   L8   ,,   ,,   ◖   ,,   ,,   (8) – (10)

  ,,   ,,   ,,   9   ,,   ,,   ♭   ,,   ,,   (L12) – (L2)

The deviations of the LB axis scale are:

the arc around L10 deviating toward ♮ consisting of: (∞) – (L3)

  ,,   ,,   ,,   2   ,,   ,,   ◖   ,,   ,,   (L2) – (L4)

  ,,   ,,   ,,   L3   ,,   ,,   ▶   ,,   ,,   (6) – (8)

  ,,   ,,   ,,   L4   ,,   ,,   ▮   ,,   ,,   (0) – (L9)

  ,,   ,,   ,,   8   ,,   ,,   ▯   ,,   ,,   (L8) – (L10)

  ,,   ,,   ,,   L9   ,,   ,,   ◁   ,,   ,,   (12) – (2)

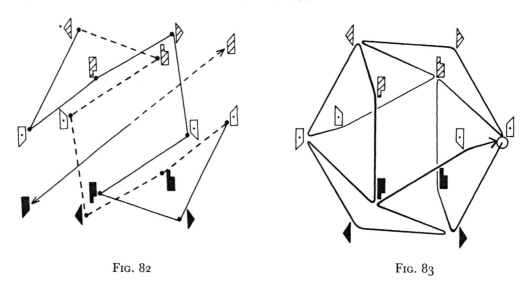

FIG. 82   FIG. 83

These deviations of each scale together form the peripheral standard scale which we also call *primary scale*.* (Fig. 82 shows the primary scale of the LB axis, ⋯ .) The primary scale was a name given to these movement sequences by Rudolf Laban, because they were the first he discovered in investigating the harmonic relationships of movement. From this it can be seen that he found the more complex form first and gradually clarified its simpler components, whereas in this section of our study we have used the reverse method.

In contrast to the equator, the primary scale is composed of the *second* inclinations of the volutes of the scale to which it belongs. It contains those elements found in the to and fro swaying in the various diagonals, characteristic of the untrained body and mind (*see* Chapter VII).

* Some readers will be acquainted with the numbering of the twelve corner points of the icosahedron with which Laban at one time worked experimentally. He then intended to establish the LB primary scale as the fundamental one to which all configurations belonging to the same axis are numerically related. The numbering in relation to the LB axis (, ⋯ ,) is as follows:

$$\flat = 1, \quad = 2, \quad = 3, \quad = 4, \quad = 5, \quad = 6,$$
$$= 7, \quad = 8, \quad = 9, \quad = 10, \quad = 11, \quad = 12.$$

The introduction of another axis would then require an explanation as to how it is related to the original one, whether mirrored, or echoed, etc., whilst the numerical relationships in each case remains the same in themselves, the numerals in relation to the scaffolding of the icosahedron change their places.

Apart from the two scales, the equator and the primary or peripheral standard scale which both consist of peripheral inclinations only, there exist other peripheral trace-forms which to a large extent are repetitions of transversal trace-forms.

Peripheral reflections of the transversal standard scale

It may be interesting to note, although perhaps more from a theoretical than a practical point of view, that the four transversal standard scales also find their reflections in the peripherals. They do not, however, occur in their proper order; the individual volutes of each scale are here linked by peripheral dimensions. The sequence of RA as a peripheral scale, starting ♯ is:

$$(2) - (3) - (h) - (4) - (5) - (l) - (6) - (7) - (b) -$$
$$(8) - (9) - (d) - (10) - (11) - (r) - (12) - (1) - (f) \text{ (Fig. 83)}.$$

that of RB, as a peripheral scale, starting ♮ is:

$$(o) - (8) - (r) - (L9) - (Lo) - (f) - (5) - (L6) - (d) -$$
$$(\infty) - (2) - (1) - (L3) - (L\infty) - (b) - (11) - (L12) - (h).$$

(NOTE: the letters r, l, h, d, f, b, stand for dimensional directions to right, left, high, deep, forward, backward, respectively and indicate here peripheral dimensions since they are set in brackets.)

3. SEQUENCES OF PERIPHERALS LEADING TO CONFIGURATIONS OTHER THAN SCALES

Peripheral three-rings

We have seen that two three-rings circle around each diagonal, having that diagonal as their axis. Around each end of this diagonal we now find a repetition of one of the three-rings as a peripheral three-ring. For instance: around the RA diagonal we established the three-rings L2 – L3 – L∞; L8 – L9 – Lo. Around the lower end of this diagonal we find, starting from ♭, the peripheral ring (L2) – (L3) – (L∞), and round the upper end, commencing from ♮, (L8) – (L9) – (Lo) (Fig. 84). We also notice that the diagonal pierces through the centre of each peripheral ring, and that when we move along the six deflected transversal inclinations of this diagonal (namely along the RA axis scale) we connect the two

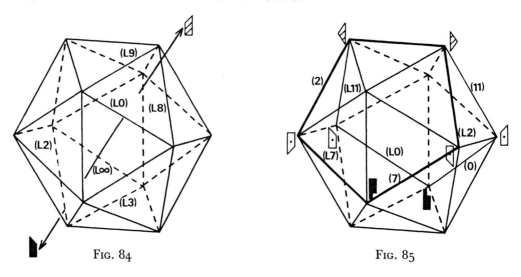

FIG. 84   FIG. 85

peripheral triangles by the to and fro movements of this scale. Thus we gain the following survey of harmonic relations:

(a) a diagonal is taken as the *axis*:
(b) six deflected transversal inclinations of the axis (*cluster or axis scale*)
(c) connect two polar triangles (*two peripheral three-rings*)
(d) which are reflections of two parallel triangles surrounding the axis nearer its centre (*two transversal three-rings*)
(e) and both of these are encircled by six peripheral inclinations (*girdle or equator scale*).

Five-rings

Without a transversal counterpart but interesting as a movement experience are the *five-rings*, in which we meet for the first time an inclusion of the dimensionals in the harmonic relations. A dimensional is taken as the basis of each five-ring, and by this we can best recognise them. For instance, let us take the peripheral r/l dimension, ♭ ... ♮. From this hangs a trace-form passing through the zone in front of the body which resembles a five-corned disc (pentagon) and which, apart from the peripheral dimension already mentioned, is bordered by two steep (11), (L11) and two flat (o), (Lo) peripherals (Fig. 85). Correspondingly, passing through the zone behind the body, there hangs from the same dimension another such disc bordered by two steep (2), (L2) and two flat (7), (L7) inclinations. Rising from the peripheral r/l dimension ▶ ... ◀, into the areas in front of and behind the body, are two more such pentagonal forms. That in front is bordered by steep (8), (L8) and flat (1), (L1), and that behind by steep (5), (L5) and flat (∞), (L∞). There are, therefore, four five-rings of equal structure attached to the two peripheral r/l dimensions. These rings are called flat because the presence of the r/l dimension in addition to the flat inclinations stresses the flat character rather than the steep element.

Four steep and four flowing rings correspond to these flat ones. They are attached to that dimension which determines their character. Therefore, attached to the peripheral f/b dimensions on the right of the body ⫞ ... ⫠ are two flowing circles, one passing through the upper zone of the kinesphere and the other through the lower:

The upper ring starting ⫞ via forward is:

$$(10) - (12) - (9) - (Lo) - \text{dimension (f)}.$$

The lower ring starting ⫞ via forward is:

$$(0) - (L9) - (L12) - (1) - \text{dimension (f)}.$$

Attached to the peripheral dimension f/b on the left side of the body ⫟ ... ⫛ there are two corresponding rings:

The upper ring starting ⫟ is:

$$(1) - (L12) - (L9) - (0) - \text{dimension (f)}.$$

The lower ring starting ⫟ is:

$$(Lo) - (9) - (12) - (10) - \text{dimension (f)}.$$

The steep five-rings are attached to the peripheral dimension h/d in front of and behind the body, passing through the right and left zones of the kinesphere. Starting ⫚ we have a ring on the right, following via high:

$$(L12) - (L2) - (L11) - (3) - \text{dimension (h)}$$

and one on the left via high:

$$(12) - (2) - (11) - (L3) - \text{dimension (h)}.$$

Attached to the peripheral dimension h/d behind the body, starting ⟨⟩ we have a ring on the left following via high:

$$(L3) - (11) - (2) - (12) - \text{dimension (h)}$$

and one on the left via high:

$$(3) - (L11) - (L12) - (L12) - \text{dimension (h)}.$$

Whilst the five-rings have no direct relationship to any scales, their relationship to single transversals is important (compare body zones, Chapter II). Each five-ring encircles a pentagram (*pentagrammon mystikon*) consisting of four transversal inclinations (*see* small shears) and one transversal dimension, which are parallel to those forming the outline of the ring (Fig. 86).

Apex-swings
Interesting and full of variety are the *apex-swings*, developed from the five-ring by combining in one swing the two which have a peripheral dimension in common. Both these five-rings are, however, not fully involved; the path is shortened by moving from the apex of one, which is the peak of a pyramid having the five-ring as its base, to the apex of the other. The trace-line runs as follows: we begin at the apex end via the peripheral dimension, we enter the circumference of the first ring, follow it along two inclinations until we meet the link common to both rings. This forms the transition into the second ring which we now follow again along two inclinations and finally divert our path—via the dimension corresponding to the initial one—in order to reach the apex of the second circle. This leads to the formation of spiral-like trace-forms which in many cases have great turning power. The return to the starting point is always along the transversal dimension which, so to speak, expands the spiral (*see* Fig. 87).

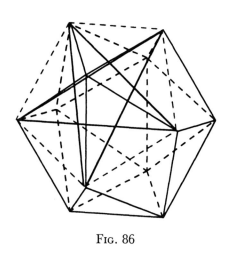

FIG. 86

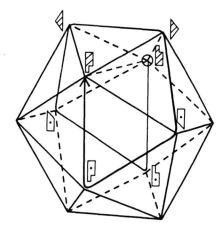

FIG. 87

EXAMPLES:

Apex-swing of two flat five-rings from ♮: (d) – (L∞) – (L5) –
(r) –
(L2) – (7) – (h) –
return to starting point: f

Apex-swing of two steep five-rings from ♮: (f) – (5) – (L9)
(d) –
(L6) – (L8) – (b)
return to starting point: r

Apex-swing of two flowing five-rings from ♭: (l) – (6) – (4)
(b) –
(7) – (L6) – (r)
return to starting point: h

Peripheral seven-rings

Before the conclusion of this section on trace-forms composed of peripherals we may briefly mention *seven-rings* as they play an important part in the harmony of movement, although an explanation of their harmonic significance falls rather outside the introductory intention of this book (*see* Chapters II, IX, X, XI).

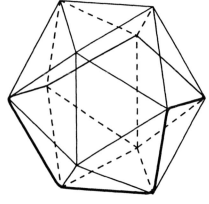

FIG. 88a

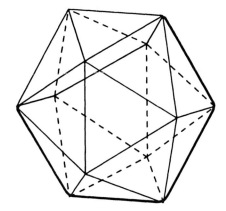

FIG. 88b

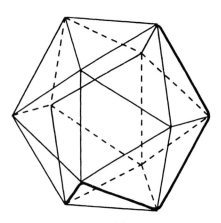

FIG. 88c

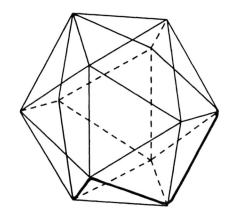

FIG. 88d

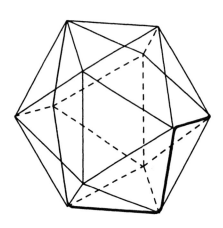

FIG. 88e

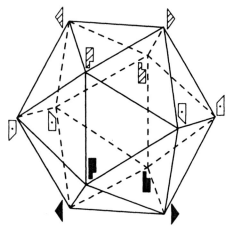

FIG. 88f

A peripheral seven-ring is composed of three links of a five-ring and four links of an equator. For example, starting ⬦:

$$(11) - (2) - (12) - (L6) - (L8) - (1) - (L12)$$

<u>five-ring part</u>   <u>equator part.</u>

The following cycle of five seven-rings represents a harmonic progression in space around the diameter ⬦ ... ▌ as axis. The first of these is, in relation to the body, symmetrically placed and we return to it after a succession of four others which induce an asymmetrical movement of the body:

(L11) – (1) – (5) – (f) – (1) – (4) – (b) } Fig. 88a

(f) – (1) – (L12) – (11) – (2) – (1) – (5) } Fig. 88b

(11) – (2) – (12) – (L6) – (L8) – (1) – (L12) } Fig. 88c

(L6) – (L8) – (L5) – (6) – (4) – (2) – (12) } Fig. 88d

(6) – (4) – (b) – (L11) – (1) – (L8) – (L5) } Fig. 88e

Fig. 88f indicates the signal-points in the icosahedron for guidance.

Mixed Sequences of Transversals and Peripherals

W E now come to movement sequences and forms which are mixtures of transversals and peripherals. These enhance a rhythmical flow of movement, and in recognising the law according to which the interchange takes place we shall also find some of the divergences explained which occur when beginners attempt to master scales and other organised movement sequences.

1. IN SCALE FORM (DEVIATION SCALES)

Let us, first of all, look at the *deviation scales* which come into being when the A- and B-Scales are performed in a freely swinging manner. The transition from one diagonal into the other (volutes) makes a great demand on the ability of the body to adjust itself to the new inclination. This is not always easily attained and requires a certain amount of movement intensity. Therefore, the body likes to take an easy way out, by following the combined forces of gravity and momentum. Before transiting into the new diagonal, the movement, like a pendulum, swings back into the previous diagonal, and then slings towards the final goal. The original inclination of the second transversal of the volute (tertiary deflected) has been transformed into a diameter (primary deflected, or plane-diagonal) which with its two-dimensional quality gives to the body more stability than the three-dimensionally inclined transversal. For instance, when we perform the volute 2 – 3 in a freely swinging manner we shall observe that the active right side limbs rebound, after the impact of 2 on point ▌, by travelling with (1) to the point ⟨. Then the transversal 3 is transformed into the diameter of the right-left plane, by slinging across from ⟨ to ⟩, which is the endpoint of 3. Thus a marked change of the original trace-form has occurred through the insertion of a peripheral.

It has been observed that this change is frequently made by beginners who have not yet been sufficiently trained to enable them to perform a smooth transition from one diagonal into the other. It has also been observed that women, when wishing to accentuate the male character of the B-Scale, nearly always use these deviations, whilst men use them in performing the A-Scale, possibly because the particular paths offer greater opportunity for free and vigorous movement.

When discussing peripherals earlier on we already referred to their relationship to a transversal as a rebound action. In recalling this we may now easily study the paths of the deviation scales, because the inserted peripheral is always a reflection of the last transversal but one in the sequence. The scales are as follows:

RA Volutes   2 – (1) – (3 transformed into diameter) 〕... 〔
            4 – (3) – (5   ,,   ,,   ,,   ) ◗ ... 〕
            6 – (5) – (7   ,,   ,,   ,,   ) ◗ ... ◀
            8 – (7) – (9   ,,   ,,   ,,   ) ◗ ... 〔
           10 – (9) – (11   ,,   ,,   ,,   ) 〕 ... ◗
           12 – (11) – (1   ,,   ,,   ,,   ') ◀ ... ◗

(Fig 89 illustrates half of the above scale. Compare also with Fig: 66.)
LA Volutes correspondingly.

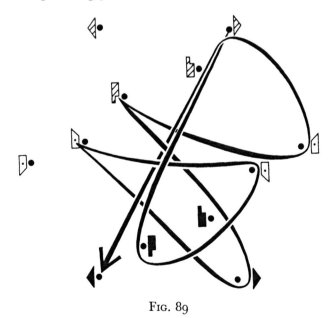

FIG. 89

RB Volutes   0 – (L12) – (*8* transformed into diameter) ▮ ... ⬚

⠀⠀⠀⠀⠀⠀⠀L9 –   (8)   – (*Lo*   „   „   „   ) ◁ ... ▶

⠀⠀⠀⠀⠀⠀⠀⠀5 –   (Lo) – (*L6*   „   „   „   ) ◱ ... ⬚

⠀⠀⠀⠀⠀⠀⠀⠀∞ –   (L6) – (*2*   „   „   „   ) ⬚ ... ▮

⠀⠀⠀⠀⠀⠀⠀L3 –   (2)   – (*L∞*   „   „   „   ) ▶ ... ◁

⠀⠀⠀⠀⠀⠀⠀11 – (L∞) – (*L12*   „   „   „   ) ⬚ ... ◱

LB Volutes correspondingly.

If we use these deviations as preparatory swings leading to an end position, we shall find that the transformed volute endings have strong positional value, because the plane-diagonals have a stabilising influence (more about this later). At this stage it need only be mentioned that the two inclinations which together form a dimensional steeple (*see* page 166) find in the same diameter their transformation. For instance, the diametral deviation for:

$$1 \text{ and } \infty \text{ is } ◁...⬚ ,$$
$$2 \text{ „ } L2 \text{ „ } ⬚...▮ ,$$
$$\text{and } 3 \text{ „ } L6 \text{ „ } ◱...⬚ .$$

We shall return to this also later in the book.

2. IN CONFIGURATIONS OTHER THAN SCALES

Two-rings

There are no other scales in which transversals and peripherals are mixed, but there are a number of configurations, of which we shall now consider the *two-rings*. These are simple movement forms which are frequently used, in parts or as a whole, in training exercises for the trunk.

Each two-ring consists of two parallel transversals connected by two peripherals, also parallel to each other. In order to make the moves 1 and 7 in succession, we must use peripheral (11) as a transition between them and between 7 and 1 we need peripheral (5). From this combination results a rectangle 1 – (11) – 7 – (5) (Fig. 90).

All parallel inclinations can similarly be connected to form such rectangles, called two-rings, as they contain only two transversals which through their direction and counter direction give the feeling of going and returning. (They are mostly performed in a swinging manner.) The 24 transversals can, therefore, be formed into twelve two-rings:

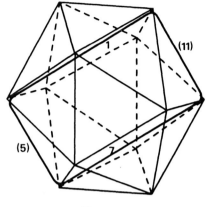

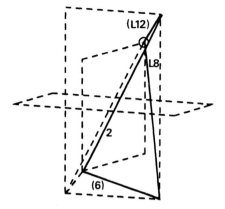

FIG. 90   FIG. 91

Flat: $1 - (11) - 7 - (5)$
             $L1 - (L11) - L7 - (L5)$
             $\infty - (L2) - 0 - (L8)$
             $L\infty - (2) - Lo - (8)$
Steep: $2 - (L6) - 8 - (L12)$
             $L2 - (6) - L8 - (12)$
             $5 - (3) - 11 - (9)$
             $L5 - (L3) - L11 - (L9)$
Flowing: $3 - (1) - 9 - (7)$
             $L3 - (L1) - L9 - (L7)$
             $6 - (0) - 12 - (\infty)$
             $L6 - (L\infty) - L12 - (L\infty)$

Four-rings

A variation of the two-rings are the *four-rings*, which consist of two transversals and two peripherals, like the two-rings; they are, however, not parallel in pairs, but have only the same character (flat, steep, or flowing) in pairs. They gain their shape by the introduction of the dimensional plane which is reached with the first transversal as a brake, throwing the movement back into the zone through which it came. For instance: of the two-ring $8 - (L12) - 2 - (L6)$ we perform $(L12) - 2$, and in doing this, reach the forward-backward plane in point ⌐. Instead of continuing with $(L6)$, as in the two-ring, we are thrown back by this plane into (6) and then return to the starting position   with L8 (Fig. 91). $(6) - L8$ and $(L12) - 2$ can be

14

recognised as halves of the two-rings (6) – L8 – (12) – L2 on the one hand and (L6) – 8 – (L12) – 2 on the other. Four-rings, therefore, are combinations of two halves of two different two-rings. In this way we can form four steep, four flat and four flowing four-rings:

steep four-rings: 2 –   (6) – L8 – (L12)
                    L2 – (L6) – 8 – (12)
                     5 – (L3) – L11 – (9)
                    L5 –   (3) – 11 – (L9)

flat four-rings: 1 – (L2) – 0 – (5)
                    L1 –   (2) – L0 – (L5)
                     ∞ – (11) – 7 – (L8)
                    L∞ – (L11) – L7 – (8)

flowing four-rings: 3 – (L0) – L12 – (7)
                    L3 –   (0) – 12 – (L7)
                     6 – (L1) – L9 – (∞)
                    L6 –   (1) – 9 – (L∞)

A characteristic of the four-rings is that they are situated only in one half of the kinesphere. The steep ones are in the right or left half, the flat in the front or back half and the flowing in the top or bottom half. As a movement experience they challenge, through their more defined trace-forms, greater intensity than the two-rings. (More about their harmonic relations later on.)

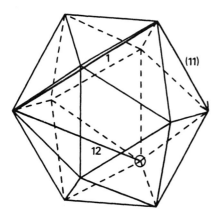

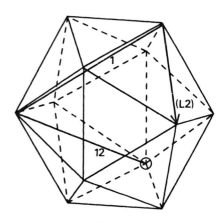

FIG. 92a   FIG. 92b

Augmented three-rings

Another combination of transversals and peripherals has to be mentioned: *the augmented three-rings*. These arise when a three-ring is not closed by its vol-link but is drawn out into a widening spiral. Each volute has two peripheral possibilities for such augmentation. Both have the same spatial character as the vol-link which they replace, but they belong to different diagonals. The peripheral following the volute is in one case that which would lead over into a two-ring and the other is that which would lead into a four-ring: the augmentations are as follows (the order is taken according to the transversal standard scales):

2 – 3 – (1) (two-ring)	8 – 9 – (7) (two-ring)
2 – 3 – (Lo) (four-ring)	8 – 9 – (L∞) (four-ring)
4 – 5 – (3) (two-ring)	10 – 11 – (9) (two-ring)
4 – 5 – (L3) (four-ring)	10 – 11 – (L9) (four-ring)
6 – 7 – (5) (two-ring)	12 – 1 – (11) (two-ring) (Fig. 92a)
6 – 7 – (L8) (four-ring)	12 – 1 – (L2) (four-ring) (Fig. 92b)

LA correspondingly.

Volutes of RB with their three-ring augmentations:

0 – 8 – (L12) (two-ring)	∞ – 2 – (L6) (two-ring)
0 – 8 – (12) (four-ring)	∞ – 2 – (6) (four-ring)
L9 – Lo – (8) (two-ring)	L3 – L∞ – (2) (two-ring)
L9 – Lo – (L5) (four-ring)	L3 – L∞ – (L11) (four-ring)
5 – L6 – (Lo) (two-ring)	11 – L12 – (L∞) (two-ring)
5 – L6 – (1) (four-ring)	11 – L12 – (7) (four-ring)

LB correspondingly.

Mixed seven-rings

An interesting series of configurations which consist of a combination of transversals and peripherals are the *mixed seven-rings* which will briefly be mentioned. The two fundamental movement shapes,* that of penetrating space and that of embracing it, create trace-forms which show sections of an axis-scale combined with sections of its equator. Two peripherals link the axis-scale and equator sections with each other at either end so as to form a ring.

* See attitudes and arabesques in *The Mastery of Movement* by R. Laban, pp. 89–90.

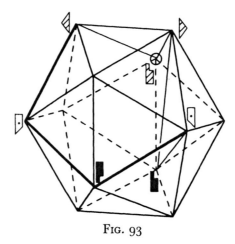

FIG. 93

Examples of mixed seven-rings of RA axis (the first of these is shown in Fig. 93) are:

$$(L12) - L11 - L12 - (7) - (10) - (8) - (6)$$

transitory   transitory
link   Axis   link   Equator

leading to   leading to three
line-like position   dimensional position
(arabesque)   (attitude)

$$(0) - L12 - 0 - (5) - (8) - (6) - (4)$$

$$(L5) - 0 - L5 - (3) - (6) - (4) - (2)$$

There are six mixed seven-rings related to each of the four axis-scales. Examples of LB axis are:

$$(L3) - 2 - L3 - (0) - (L\infty) - (L5) - (9)$$

$$(L4) - L3 - L4 - (L8) - (L5) - (9) - (Lo)$$

$$(8) - L4 - 8 - (12) - (9) - (Lo) - (L11)$$

SECTION V

Harmonic Relations

WITH the movement sequences shown so far we have attempted to give a survey of the fundamental material and its organisation. There now remains the task of explaining some of the harmonic relations and of expounding and deepening the meaning of what has been said. As we have seen, there is an amazing order which seems never to be disturbed. This order can be recognised everywhere, so also in all forms of dance or any other organised movement, skill or style. Justification for the proposition that the icosahedron is an appropriate scaffolding for the consideration of a harmony of movement has been attempted in the first part of the book (*see* Chapter X). As mentioned before, it was not in the first place knowledge of the factors and the relationships explained above which caused Laban to relate the movements of the human body to the icosahedron; he discovered, only after many trials and errors, an order in which he saw correspondences to the structure of that solid. The icosahedron, in fact, is a structural whole (it embraces the pentagon—dodecahedron which in turn is a dynamic complication of the cube with its octahedral kernel formed by two tetrahedra penetrating one another) which can provide a basis for comprehending the multitude of forms created by the flux of energy as it gives a means for tracing their selection and interrelations.

1. ALL INCLINATIONS ARE RELATED TO ONE SCALE

In summarising, let us first of all say something about the functions of the twenty-four main inclinations. Contrary to the first part of the book which showed a development from the peripheral standard scale (primary scale) this section will proceed from its inner reflection, the transversal standard scale. We found twelve transversal inclinations contained in this scale and six inclinations combined in its corresponding axis-scale (12 plus 6=18). The

195

relationship of the six remaining inclinations to this scale is to be found in the two three-rings around the missing diagonal, or axis.

> RA: Scale: $1 - 2 - 3 - 4 - 5 - 6 - 7 - 8 - 9 - 10 - 11 - 12$
>   Axis: $\infty - L11 - L12 - 0 - L5 - L6$
>   Two three-rings: $L2 - L3 - L\infty$; $L8 - L9 - L0$
> RB: Scale: $0 - 8 - L9 - L0 - 5 - L6 - \infty - 2 - L3 - L\infty - 11 - L12$
>   Axis: $9 - 10 - L2 - 3 - 4 - L8$
>   Two three-rings: $L5 - 6 - 7$; $L11 - 12 - 1$.

LA and LB correspondingly.

All peripheral inclinations have also a relationship to their appropriate standard scale. The peripheral counterparts of the transversal scale are to be found in the primary scale (volute beginnings) and in the equator (volute endings). In addition, the primary scale contains those peripheral inclinations which are parallel to the axis, and the parallels to the two three-rings are set as peripheral three-rings around the extremities of the missing diagonal.

Organisation into three-rings

One can also relate the twenty-four inclinations to the three-rings. Around each of the four diagonals are situated two transversal three-rings and two peripheral three-rings $(4 \times 2 \times 3 = 24)$.

Organisation into two-rings and four-rings

Likewise, all twenty-four transversals have a function in the two-rings as well as in the four-rings. We have ascertained that there are twelve two-rings and twelve four-rings. Each of these contains two transversals and two peripherals, with the result that all inclinations are contained in each of the twelve rings $(2 \times 12$ and $2 \times 12)$.

These are, of course, considerations of purely theoretical value, but they indicate the supreme order which exists in harmonious movement.

2. EACH INCLINATION IS RELATED TO EACH OF THE PRIMARY SCALES

We find yet another remarkable order in the primary circuits. This is that each primary scale shows in its division the relationship to its appropriate basic scale (A or B). This has been explained in detail earlier in the book (*see* Chapter VII).

Intervals of the primary scale

Apart from the theoretical interest in these combinations, the intervals, as explained in Chapter VII, as well as the two- four- and five-part circumventions of the transversals by curves derived from the four primary scales, are excellent material for movement-exercises. For instance, a crescendo exercise, consisting of an increasing number of peripherals circumventing a transversal, provides great possibilities for the variety of trace-forms which can be developed from a simple movement motif.

Circumvention of each transversal by several five-ring arcs

The five-rings give further possibilities of development. We have already seen that each of these rings is placed around four transversals each of which divides the ring into two parts, one consisting of two, the other of three links. In other words, each of these parts is a circumvention of a transversal. For instance, let us take the movement 1 which leads from ♩ to ♭ in a flat circle behind the body. We can make an arc-like gesture by using the two-part circumvention of (8) – (r) or the three-part one of (L7) – (1) – (L8). But the transversal lies also within one of the flowing five-rings above the centre which gives us the two-part deviation of (∞) – (L3) and the three-part one of (f) – (1) – (L12). Therefore there are four different possibilities of circumventing a transversal by means of the five-rings, which are identifiable thus:

(*a*) a two-part arc including a peripheral dimension;
(*b*) a three-part arc including a peripheral dimension;

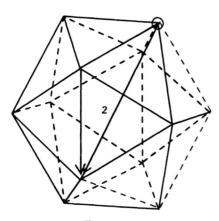

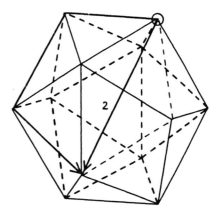

FIG. 94*a*   FIG. 94*b*

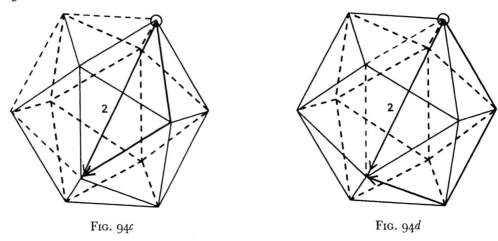

FIG. 94c   FIG. 94d

(c) a two-part arc consisting of peripheral inclinations only;
(d) a three-part arc consisting of peripheral inclinations only.

Figs. 94a–d illustrate these aspects in relation to transversal 2.

The two circumventions which contain dimensionals are situated on one side of the transversal and those containing inclinations on the other. This applies to all transversals in the same manner. In moving freely, these arcs are rarely clearly performed in their exact trace-form, and we therefore speak rather of two *zones* around each inclination, calling one the "dimensional zone," the other the "diagonal zone." Their significance is discussed in the next section.

Stable and Labile Relationships

1. WITHIN HARMONIC TRACE-FORMS

FINALLY, we must mention an aspect which is a most important one for the understanding of the harmonic relations between the inclinations, namely the *stable* and the *labile relationships*. "Stable" should not be taken to be static and motionless. We look upon it as that element which leads movement to quiescence and stillness, which causes a movement theme to fade out and to find a conclusion in itself without anticipation of a new theme. Spatially, its opposing tensions firmly wield the equilibrium of forces.

Two-ring relationships (stable)

With the term "labile" we designate a state which strongly promotes continuity and is charged with movement intensity, thus creating ever-new movements which do not find a conclusion in themselves. It is promoted by smooth and easy transitions between spatial directions and has a pliant structure. If we now investigate the two-rings from this point of view we meet an interesting harmonic relation which exists between a set of three two-rings. For instance:

SET I:

First two-ring: 1 – (11) – 7 – (5)
Second two-ring: 5 – (3) – 11 – (9)
Third two-ring: 3 – (1) – 9 – (7)
First two-ring: 1 – (11) – 7 – (5)

We find that these three two-rings are related to another by the peripherals which in each following ring have become the transversals and after three changes the first ring is again established. The same can be observed in the following:

SET II:

First two-ring:	$2 - (L6) - 6 - (L12)$
Second two-ring:	$L12 - (L\infty) - L6 - (Lo)$
Third two-ring:	$L\infty - (2) - Lo - (8)$
First two-ring:	$2 - (L6) - 8 - (L12)$

There are two corresponding sets on the other side.

We distinguish, therefore, four sets of three two-rings, each of which forms a cycle. The inclinations occurring in each cycle are situated at right angles to one another, reminding us of the system of the three-dimensional planes, only tilted towards one or other of the diagonals. Further, we observe that each two-ring cycle combines those inclinations which, in a transversal standard scale, are the first movement of a steeple and the second of a volute. Therefore each two-ring cycle belongs to a particular transversal standard scale.

Set I to: RA $\quad 1 - 3 - 5 - 7 - 9 - 11$

LA $\quad L1 - L3 - L5 - L7 - L9 - L11$

Set II to: RB $\quad 8 - Lo - L6 - 2 - L\infty - L12$

LB $\quad L8 - 0 - 6 - L2 - \infty - 12$

From the point of view of movement composition, these inclinations are isolated from one another, i.e. within the same cycle there is no freedom of change from one two-ring to any other without introducing a foreign element as a transition. Each ring is directly connected only with one other one. There is, therefore, no variability.

For the time being we shall use the term "stable relationships" only to signify a rigidity arising on the one hand from this isolation of inclinations, and on the other, from their situation to one another at right angles which is of great importance to the stable character of their combined structure. A little further on, we shall point out how these inclinations appear as stabilising elements in scales as well as in other organised sequences.

In contrast to the stable relationships there are labile ones which in each scale appear as the second movement of a steeple (or first of a volute), and together they form angles of $72°$ and $108°$.

Intersections on diagonal directions (labile)

We have already become acquainted with the peripheral counterparts of the labile transversals when considering the girdles in which they appear in a particular order forming the equator scales.

These transversals are for

RA: 2 – 4 – 6 – 8 – 10 – 12
LA: L2 – L4 – L6 – L8 – L10 – L12
RB: 0 – L9 – 5 – ∞ – L3 – L11
LB: L0 – 9 – L5 – L∞ – 3 – 11

Three of these labile inclinations intersect one another at one point on the diagonal (the missing diagonal) of its respective scale and the other three at another point on the same diagonal, at the opposite end:

2 – 6 – 10 intersect at	}	RA Diagonal (Fig. 95)
4 – 8 – 12 ,, ,,	}	
L2 – L6 – L10 ,, ,,	}	LA Diagonal
L4 – L8 – L12 ,, ,,	}	
11 – ∞ – L9 ,, ,,	}	RB Diagonal
5 – 0 – L3 ,, ,,	}	
L11 – L∞ – 9 ,, ,,	}	LB Diagonal
L5 – L0 – 3 ,, ,,	}	

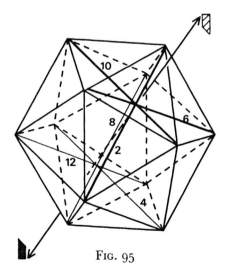

FIG. 95

If we extract these labile connections from the tangle of all the other inclinations we find that each labile system shapes into a rhombohedron which resembles a cube squashed in the direction of the missing diagonal.

It is also remarkable that each of the labile transversals leads to its respective girdle where it meets the peripheral counterparts of the two inclinations intersecting it, namely those with which it is closely related. For instance, moving along inclination 2 to backward-deep, the movement can be continued within this system with a peripheral 6 or 10. This fact makes a choice of continuation possible and, together with angles less rigid than in the stable system, the labile quality is enhanced.

Survey of inclinations in relation to their function

In summarising this it may be said that each inclination has in one of the scales either a labile or a stable character according to the part it plays within a volute and a steeple, i.e. whether it occurs as a first movement into a new diagonal or as a second one.

From this it may become clear that, since each inclination is present in two scales, it also has both a *stabilising and a mobilising function:*

Inclination:	Stable:	Labile:	Inclination:	Stable:	Labile:
1	RA	LA	8	RB	RA
2	RB	RA	9	RA	LB
3	RA	LB	10	LA	RA
4	LA	RA	11	RA	RB
5	RA	RB	12	LB	RA
6	LB	RA	0	LA	RB
7	RA	LA	∞	LB	RB

Left side correspondingly.

We have already established the following characteristics:

For stability:
1. Angle of 90°.
2. No variability.
3. The whole system consisting of unrelated planes, similar to the dimensional planes.

For mobility:
1. Angle of 72° or 108°.
2. Variability.
3. Whole system shapes into a rhombohedron. Transversals intersect in two sets of three. Peripherals form equator scale.

Deviation scales

Our task is now to recognise the relationships of stability and mobility in movement. Let us first re-examine the deviation scales. We had found that those inclinations which were to proceed into a new diagonal had transformed their three-dimensional value into a two-dimensional one and become a diameter. They represent the stable inclinations within a scale which, through their closer relationship to a dimension, tend to stabilise the movement and to bring it to an ending position. The labile inclinations have a preparatory function and remain unchanged in their three-dimensional value.

Three-ring augmentations

As the next example for the difference between labile and stable movement we mention the two kinds of *three-ring augmentations*, which differ in this respect. Let us take for instance, $2 - 3 - (1)$ and $2 - 3 - (Lo)$. When moving along these trace-forms we shall feel that $2 - 3 - (1)$ means the fading of the movement theme, whilst $2 - 3 - (Lo)$ doubtlessly suggest recharging as it leads over into a new movement theme. The same applies to all three-ring augmentations. The stable augmentation continues with the original character of the movement curve, either gathering or scattering into an *ouvert* whilst the labile augmentation changes the character by reversing the original tendency by a *tortillé* (*see* Chapter VIII). In addition, the stable augmentation always remains in the same diagonal as the first inclination of the volute—whilst the labile augmentation leads into a third diagonal (that of the axis). Together, all these facts cause the labile augmentations to contain much more movement intensity than the stable ones.

Four-rings

The same can be said of the *four-rings*, where, in contrast to the two-rings, we have two labile and only two stable transitions. This results in the formation of a three-dimensional shape differing from the monotony of the plane-like two-ring, and giving a richer movement experience through its plastic spatial structure.

The labile transition always occurs at the end of a transversal when the movement enters the peripheral path. A greater movement intensity is here experienced which again fades away on entering the next transversal because that transition is a stable one.

Stable and labile zones through circumvention of transversals by five-rings

When we consider stability and mobility, we find that the *zones* which we had established in connection with the circumvention made by five-rings, are of great importance. There we distinguished between a dimensional and a diagonal zone. If we now study more closely the kind of deviations which commonly occur when people move freely along trace-forms of volutes we find that they tend to prefer these detours. (There is, of course, always the exception, which is of no great importance, especially when the mover tends towards the grotesque.) The first volute-inclination (labile) is usually taken through the diagonal or labile zone, whilst the second movement (stable) finds its deviation through the dimensional or stable zone. The flowing inclinations, however, do not seem to correspond exactly to this rule, but it has been observed that only the inclination 3 seems often to go against it. Likewise ∞ and o have at times been found to be exceptions:

1 in RA stable zone;	in LA as L10 labile zone;
2 in RA labile zone;	in RB stable zone;
3 in RA labile zone;	in LB mostly labile zone;
(only when turning in the stable zone)	
4 in RA labile zone;	in LA as L7 stable zone;
5 in RA stable zone;	in RB labile zone;
6 in RA labile zone;	in LB mostly also labile zone;
7 in RA stable zone;	in LA as L4 labile zone;
8 in RA labile zone;	in RB stable zone;
9 in RA mostly stable zone;	in LB labile zone;
10 in RA labile zone;	in LA as L1 stable zone;
11 in RA stable zone;	in RB labile zone;
12 in RA labile zone;	in LB stable zone;
∞ in RB mostly labile zone;	in LB always labile zone;
o in RB large stable zone;	in LB stable zone.

As already explained, these are the kind of deviations which can generally be recognised. Divergences can be seen in certain types of movers who prefer the detours belonging to the deviation scale, especially when the expressive element dominates over the form-giving one in the movement.

If we combine the various zones of the volutes in different ways, e.g. two labile or two stable zones, variations of trace-forms for a volute are created such as *ouverts*, *tortillés*, etc. This again provides rich material for educating the dancer in the appreciation of form; a new feeling will be awakened for the deviations of the different inclinations of flat, steep and flowing.

2. THE INFLUENCE OF DIAGONALS ON ONE ANOTHER

Another interesting example of the use of labile and stable zones is the following for which the diagonal ◊ ... ▌ with its inclinations 1– L3 – 8 towards the upward end and 7 – L9 – 2 towards the downward end will serve us. Inclination 1 has its dimensional zone in front of the body, with strong accentuation of a left to right movement. The zone as a whole is bordered by a trace-line ◊ ... ◊ ... ◊ and ◊ ... ◊ ... ◊ ... ◊ and encloses the triangle ◊ ... ◊ ... ◊ which surrounds the diagonal direction ◊ (Fig. 96a). This is separated from the diagonal direction ◊, towards which the transversal 1 is inclined, by a right-left dimension (compare the diagonals in the cube). In movement we experience this dimensional zone as a deflection of the diagonal direction ◊ by the diagonal direction ◊, which at first attracts and then pushes the movement to the right. A similar experience we can have with 7, the only difference being that the opposite ends of the two diagonals become active; i.e. ▌ of 7, ▌ attracts, and then pushes to the left.

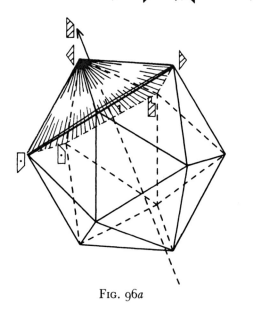

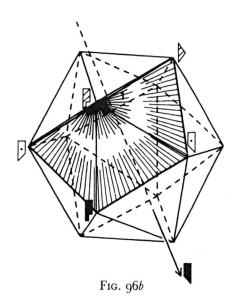

FIG. 96a   FIG. 96b

In moving, this deflection of one diagonal by another is most easily felt if the whole body is first tilted into the diagonal, in our case ⧄ ... ▌, and then by a propulsion of the centre of the body a right arm gesture is made into the flat inclination. In this way it is, so to speak, pushed by the dimension leading to the right, whilst the leg is pushed by the dimension leading to the left.

Alternatively we can feel that it is not only this dimensional push which causes the deflection, but that there is also a possibility of a pull. This pulling deflection occurs in the labile zones, which is for inclination 1 behind the body and bordered by a trace-line ⧄ ... ▌ ... ⧄ ... ♭, and ⧄ ... ⧄ ... ♭ (Fig. 96b). For example, let us start at ⧄ but this time with the right arm crossed behind the body. We can clearly recognise how the inclination 1 is now diverted towards the diagonal ▌ (the first peripheral of the three-link labile detour belongs to this diagonal). The movement is first pulled towards the right and then released on the right side, towards the end of inclination 1 (Fig. 97).

When we consider the steep deflection of the diagonal direction ⧄ we find that in the labile zone the diagonal direction ⧄ pulls upward and, in the stable zone the diagonal direction ▌ pushes upward. The steep deflection of ▌ is pushed from ⧄ downward (stable detour) and pulled from ▌ downward (labile detour).

In the flowing deflection of ⧄ it is ⧄ that pushes forward (stable detour) and ▌ that pulls forward (labile detour). For the counter-direction of the inclination it is ▌ that pushes (stable detour) and ⧄ that pulls (labile detour).

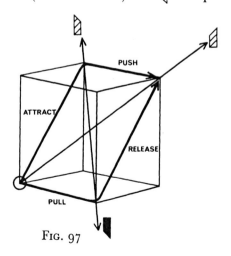

FIG. 97

If we present these relationships in a cube we find that both the labile and the stable characteristics are provoked by *one* diagonal other than that of the inclination, and that the pulling and pushing of the two directions of an inclination are caused by that *one* diagonal, thus establishing an inter-relationship between the two diagonals.

Each diagonal has this kind of deflecting relationship to every other diagonal. These considerations are important because they help to free movement from all-too-rigid theoretical conceptions and enrich dynamic qualities. They are also important in the notation of movement sequences, because they facilitate the notating of curving movements by deviation signs, added to those of main inclinations.

SECTION VII

Survey of Elements Restraining or Promoting Flux of Movement

To summarise let us recall once more which movement elements have a furthering or a restricting influence on the flux of movement, because this problem has repeatedly occurred in our study of space-harmony. We found that the dimensionals always induce restriction; in the purely linear dimension no natural movement is possible, in the dimensional-plane movement is possible but only restrictedly. In contrast to this is the pure diagonal, which is charged with movement intensity to such a degree that the movement flows on in an unrestrained manner. Therefore:

1. *Dimension=restraining.*
   Diagonal=promoting the flux of movement.

We also found that the transition from one diagonal into the other enhances movement intensity, whilst the remaining in the same diagonal induces a calming down of movement (similar to the fading away of the momentum in a pendulum swing). Therefore:

2. *Remaining in the same diagonal=restraining.*
   Transition from one diagonal to another=promoting.

Further, we can observe a difference in the influence of plane-like or plastic trace-forms. Plane-like movements induce calming down, whilst those using three-dimensional paths are rousing:

3. *Plane-like shapes=restraining flux.*
   Plastic shapes=promoting flux.

It is also important to ascertain if a movement sequence returns to its starting point or if it progresses in space:

4. *Returning to the starting point=restraining flux.*
   Progressing in space=promoting flux.

We already found in detail that there are stable relationships and labile relationships.

5. *Stable relationships=restraining flux.*
   Labile relationships=promoting flux.

Of importance for the intensity of movement is the use of peripherals or transversals:

6. *Peripherals are restraining; transversals are promoting.*

Lastly we mention rhythm, of which very little has been said. It is undoubtedly convincing that a regular rhythm (2/4 time) is of a more monotonous quality than an irregular one (3 or 5 time) from which we conclude that:

7. *Regular rhythm is restraining; irregular rhythm is promoting.*

Let us finish with a survey of the most important factors, set forth in detail above, which influence the flux of movement through their restraining or promoting elements.

	Restraining	*Promoting*
Steeples:	one diagonal only plane-like shape regular rhythm	passing through opposite zones of space transversals only
Volutes:	plane-like shape regular rhythm	two different diagonals transversals only
Transversal three-rings:	plane-like shape return to starting point	three different diagonals irregular rhythm transversals only

Equator: (girdle)	return to starting point peripherals only	three different diagonals plastic shape labile relationships between links
Peripheral three-rings:	plane-like shape return to starting point peripherals only	three different diagonals irregular rhythm
Five-rings:	one dimensional direction two diagonals only plane-like shape return to starting point peripherals only	continual change of diagonals labile relationships between links irregular rhythm

Apex: swings:	dimensional directions
	   (three occurrences)
	peripherals only
		four different diagonals
		continual change of diagonals
		plastic shape
		labile relationships between links
		irregular rhythm
		passing through opposite zones of
		   space

Two-rings:	accent on one diagonal plane-like shape return to starting point stable relationships regular rhythm two peripherals	two different diagonals two transversals
Four-rings:	return to starting point two stable relationships regular rhythm two peripherals	four different diagonals plastic shape two labile relationships two transversals

Index

Lightning Source UK Ltd.
Milton Keynes UK
UKOW011440110512

192383UK00001B/3/P